Past Life Regression

Exploring the Past to Heal the Present

(Learn Hypnotic Regression to Uncover Hidden Past Life Memories, Astral Projection)

Robert Miller

Published By **Andrew Zen**

Robert Miller

Past Life Regression: Exploring the Past to Heal the Present (Learn Hypnotic Regression to Uncover Hidden Past Life Memories, Astral Projection)

ISBN 978-1-998769-74-2

No part of this guidebook shall be reproduced in any form without permission in writing from the publisher except in the case of brief quotations embodied in critical articles or reviews.

Legal & Disclaimer

The information contained in this ebook is not designed to replace or take the place of any form of medicine or professional medical advice. The information in this ebook has been provided for educational & entertainment purposes only.

The information contained in this book has been compiled from sources deemed reliable, and it is accurate to the best of the Author's knowledge; however, the Author cannot guarantee its accuracy and validity and cannot be held liable for any errors or omissions. Changes are periodically made to this book. You must consult your doctor or get professional medical advice before using any of the suggested remedies, techniques, or information in this book.

Table of contents

Chapter 1: Synopsis

75% of the arena's population today believes in reincarnation. However, such notion doesn't come clean on the subject of Americans and different Westerners. Even although their hearts inform them it is actual, their brains insist on more proof.

Past lifestyles regressions are the evidence they - or maybe even you - are seeking out. Have you ever skilled a sense of déjà vu on your existence? Most human beings do - and extra than as soon as at that. Such reports produce shiny pics in your mind that you are feeling like it did appear to you. The query is, why can't it be actual?

The Basics

There are also properly and bad goals that occur time and again once more. It's simpler for children to recognize the matters they suppose, feel, and feature achieved within the beyond which are nevertheless of their minds. As a infant's mind isn't always filled with ideas approximately what is real and what isn't always, it doesn't automatically reject what it sees as fake. As for after they tell the adults approximately it, this is a whole other factor! Because kid's minds also are impressionable, telling them repeatedly that what they may be seeing is not actual will subsequently lead them to think in a certain manner.

You are no longer a infant, but it will nevertheless be difficult so as to exchange or even think in a different way. However, there is a lot to be able to revel in in case you even reflect onconsideration on beyond lifestyles regressions and reincarnation as a minimum a little bit. There are things approximately your lifestyles that you in no way idea you knew. Seeing how your past lives have fashioned you can additionally make you greater at peace with yourself.

To open yourself to these possibilities will take time and effort. This e-book is supposed to make your adventure of self-discovery pass lots quicker, although, so don't worry about that.

It's critical to keep an open mind as you move from one page to the next. Don't just reject some thing due to the fact your thoughts tells you it doesn't make sense. Things in this global don't make experience.

If you insist in limiting yourself to only rational possibilities, life will progressively lose its that means, its magic---or even its importance.

If you keep proscribing yourself to rational options, lifestyles will lose its magic, its that means, or even its value.

Everyone can study this book. It doesn't remember what your faith is, how vintage you are, or how you watched of yourself. God does not care. As a end result, quite a few human beings suppose that there's most effective one God who regulations over all of them.

Only the name changes. This e book will not alternate your faith. There is a good hazard that, then again, you will alternate the way you see the arena, your life, and your self.

You can start changing your lifestyles right now with the aid of embracing your past and mastering the way to alternate your present and future, each now and within the destiny.

Chapter 2: Memories are Not Infallible

Synopsis

Considering that maximum of us neglect matters that took place or consider things otherwise from how they happened, recollections must now not be depended on. Some humans even remember humans they have by no means met or locations they have in no way been. People can keep in mind matters that by no means passed off, or perhaps they did, however to a person else. This can make it difficult to parent out if recollections are genuine or no longer.

Young kids depend heavily on their memories to study. Still, the memories made earlier than they'd their 2d birthday are lost by the brain in blurry early life amnesia. As we pass about our lives, the reminiscences we have made assist us are expecting and put together for future activities, actions, and encounters. Even even though it isn't as vital on its very own, it allows us to conform to the one-of-a-kind conditions we are facing in our every day lives.

Memories Define Personality

You can tell your pals thrilling stories and say such things as, "I'm no longer the sort of individual who does that." This shows which you are the use of your recollections as a reference point or as the basis in your conclusion approximately how you'll act in a certain way.

Memory additionally makes us think that our lives are logical and that nothing is introduced or taken far from them. The truth is that our lives are irrational and incoherent. When we swap memories, we can see that lying is inevitable. Most of the time, we miss lots information and make up matters to make our memories seem greater steady. Over time, we keep in mind the tales we advised and trust them authentic.

In this example, the reminiscences are not real.

Research suggests that our earliest reminiscences are very questionable. Experiments show that a infant's recollections are higher than an older infant's. When we are 5 years antique, we can recall some of the matters we did in our early life. When we have been younger, our reminiscences were probable made up via the tales we have been advised, and we internalized them and made them our own.

Memory is a process that adjustments all of the time. It calls for remembering occasions or reports, that is a good deal work because no mind shops memories. We make our records as we move about our lives. When we come upon new information, we make it into a new story through combining it with our reminiscences.

Some human beings assume that sexually abused youngsters who've intellectual illnesses are probable to have had repressed reminiscences that precipitated them to have those mental ailments. Some examples of this had been while victims said they had rediscovered reminiscences of infant abuse. On the opposite hand, psychologists and therapists say that these reminiscences are not true. They say that therapists ought to be careful and phenomenological when they speak to their patients, not influencing or encouraging their patients to recall matters that by no means happened.

Chapter 3: Fatalism is not the Correct

Approach Synopsis

Fatalism isn't always the right way to address matters

As a result, people accept their fates due to the fact they assume they are already set in stone. This is referred to as "fatalism." Fatalism is regularly believed to agree with that the destiny will constantly give up incorrect.

People who trust in destiny generally tend to think that they're powerless and cannot do some thing to change their destiny.

In fatalism, there may be the idea that human beings ought to be given their fate instead of combat or alternate it. Most human beings who have this philosophy come from human beings who have been taught loads approximately predestination or who suppose they can predict what will show up in life.

However, this isn't the proper way to stay your life. Everyone could make his future and now not allow what he thinks will make him do terrible things.

Fatalism and the Unpredictability of People

All people have extraordinary personalities, so this may lead to numerous activities of their lives. Each person has their own set of beliefs, views, movements, and reactions, which can be very exceptional from every different.

They will all have an effect on your future, how you believe you studied, or what you think about existence. This isn't a joke. Fatalists need to apprehend that unpredictability results in no longer exactly what fatalism teaches.

Fatalists don't like social conditions.

Fatalists don't try to trade the direction of destiny, and they don't want to. This is why they don't commonly get too enthusiastic about assembly new people and learning them. They could as a substitute watch and try to discern out what's going to happen ultimately than deliver their own opinion. They assume that they can not change what has already been determined and do not have the electricity to do anything approximately it.

They also generally tend to keep away from non-public relationships with different humans because they handiest need to see if their anticipated outcome will show up or now not. However, it's miles essential to keep in mind that guy is a social animal. He desires to engage with different human beings to develop and increase. Shy away from socializing

This isn't desirable if you want to stay your lifestyles absolutely.

Make sure you do not end up a fatalist

It may be hard for fatalists to peer the world essentially. People who have these beliefs want to just accept that matters can happen that are not what they expect. Having hindsight can be appropriate for other human beings because they look for advice when they make decisions. Still, it shouldn't have an effect on how properly a person's lifestyles is typical. A fatalist who wants to change his views should receive that his destiny can be based totally on what he has accomplished inside the beyond. These reports are based totally on what took place, this means that that they will be different for everybody who has one in all them.

Chapter 4: The Law of Cause and Effect,

Karma Synopsis

It's called the Law of Cause and Effect or Karma.

When talking approximately Karma, many people think that this happens due to something horrible that occurred inside the beyond. This isn't true at all.

However, the concept of Karma is greater than that. It talks approximately the herbal law of purpose and impact in simple phrases. You get again what you provide. Thus, your movements will lead to the Karma with a view to come into your life in a while, which is why you must do what you can now. When you do something true, you may count on your Karma to be in a better mood. At the identical time, terrible Karma will come into your existence while you do bad things.

Phases of Karma

You won't continually be punished or rewarded for what you do due to the fact Karma is the law of purpose and effect. People undergo unique degrees of the law of Karma, which enables matters stability out in the global. To understand Karma, you want to recognize about the exclusive degrees it is going through.

Sanchita Karma is the first phase of Karma that is notion of because the seed or very first stage. This kind of Karma covers the Karma that someone has triggered in his beyond and cutting-edge existence.

The 2nd segment of Karma is the only that makes the seeds, so that is the one. We make the Kriyamana Karma while we do things each day. Those seeds will grow together with those performed in the beyond and the subsequent existence.

There is a call for the ultimate phase of Karma. It's known as Prarabdha Karma. People undergo this section each day, and it is part of the Karma that has already grown old.

Prarabdha is a form of yoga.

In the stages of Prarabdha karma, which you may now not even recognise approximately, you are dwelling your life now. The matters which are occurring for your lifestyles result from the seeds that have already grown that you have sown in your lifestyles.

In the beyond. If you've got bad Karma, it may come lower back to hang-out you in lots of one of a kind approaches. This type of Karma could make you feel horrific approximately yourself, depend upon others, and have awful emotions approximately your circle of relatives.

The herbal regulation of reason and effect will help you plan how you could plant effective seeds with the intention to develop into high quality Karma while the time is proper. Being a law of nature, you could stability the wrong things with the coolest ones through eliminating evil thoughts and moves and living a terrific life. "Bhakti" or "devotion" is what humans typically call this kind of mindful attention to good Karma.

Creating Good Karma

Bhakti is a manner to be conscious that your desirable deeds will always deliver you closer to God. When you turn out to be conscious that your gift Karma is the end result of your beyond existence, you have got the risk to stability the Karma to your existence and make it proper. Karma ought to not be idea of as suitable or terrible. Instead, it have to be seen as a way to cast off the awful reminiscences that might were in your beyond. You can make desirable Karma connected in your modern-day existence and deliver over into the subsequent.

Chapter 5: Lords of Karma

Synopsis

There are extraordinary Lords of Karma, and every one has a distinct role in human beings's lives.

People accept as true with that Karma became best connected to awful things, even within the beyond. This has been surpassed down from one technology till studies and professionals said an top notch aspect to Karma, which made this variation.

Good deeds are rewarded with desirable matters, which means that what the ones people say has a factor. A few extra claims have been made that there are particular lords of Karma, and each had a specific task. Here are some of the most famous lords of Karma that you have to realize about, as well.

The Lords

Paul is notion to be the grasp of the ray that stands for harmony in the middle of a combat. Many people say he turned into close to Gabriel the Archangel and that God loved him due to his kindness and goodness. There's a good risk he is one of the Lords of Karma who may be related to true matters.

Katsumi

If you want to be a terrific character, you should comply with Kathumi's advice on doing correct matters. He is likewise known as the grasp of the ray that embodies real wisdom and love from God. The 2d ray has 3 developments which might be essential for human beings to have to achieve success in existence. On the other hand, Katsumi is very worried within the lives of teachers, architects, engineers, college students, and artists, so this is why. People also say that Kathumi has skilled being a person in a few manner lots. That may be why he cares so much about the well-being of the individuals who make the world go round.

The female named Portia is the one who is the one who's the only.

The Lady Portia isn't your common female. She has to stability both judgment and mercy concurrently, which isn't always some thing that maximum humans can do. Because of this, you could discern out how important she is to humans. People who're quick to decide or criticize different people are her activity. She wants to change their minds.

People who want to spread love can use this. In light of all of this, it'd be safe to mention that she gives grace to every body on Earth.

Serapis Bay is the call of the area where human beings go to get

It may be stated that Serapis Bay is good due to the compassion and intelligence he offers to people, which makes him right. People call him the grasp of the yellow-ray, which is the 0.33 ray because he allows humans obtain perfection and independence. Most artists, philosophers, and different folks who reflect onconsideration on how the world ought to work are inquisitive about this.

Lord Gautama

Lord Gautama, better known as the Buddha, is known for his awareness to folks who ask for it. Christ is the energy of love, and Lord Gautama is knowledge because he must assist different human beings analyze.

These are the maximum well-favored lords of Karma who may be called the best guys. They are also the maximum important lords of Karma while you see what they do for the people.

Chapter 6: The Degree of Reincarnation

Leads to Self-Mastery

Synopsis

The Higher the extent of reincarnation, the extra willpower you have got.Evolutionary life is seen as a way to steadily give up the lower stages of divinity so you can reach higher levels. This is due to the fact the decrease degrees of reincarnation are a part of the evolutionary intention's journey to perfection. The better levels develop right into a soul that goes thru eons of life after which returns because it desires to incarnate all life.

Effects Of Continued Reincarnation

People who hold having reincarnations will have exceptional results.

To get out of mental and bodily planes of existence whilst the soul reincarnates into a new body, it starts by using putting its features and energies into the bodies of its new our bodies. This manner is called "infusion." It's a two-step procedure. First, the soul slowly makes its vehicle extra non secular. Then, the soul intentionally burdens the automobile to burn off antique Karma.

It receives greater tough to reincarnate as your soul progresses. This makes you observed more approximately your self because you hold getting a more enormous burden with each new incarnation. In the stop, the fourth-diploma initiate, you've got the most extensive hassle of all.

This is why the West refers to the fourth reincarnation because the "Crucifixion." In assessment, the East refers to it as the "Great Renunciation." During this enjoy, every low element is given as much as gain a better non secular revel in. The fourth stage initiate is idea to be the maximum painful of all.

The extra Karma you have, the much more likely you may get what you need. Initiate the more you need to do.

This is not real in any respect. People assume that their Karma gets simpler as they move up the evolutionary ladder. This is not authentic due to the fact a reincarnated man or woman is extra disciplined.

People who tackle more of the sector's Karma become greater initiates due to the fact they sense more of its weight. People who are authentic disciples of the law of Karma help the sector because they got here into the sector to assist. The extra superior someone is, the greater provider he does for the sector.

It doesn't matter if the individual is a 3rd-diploma initiate or now not because he can alternate his destiny. The person grows into a conscious non secular soul who serves the world wholeheartedly, controlling the law of reason and impact. Even although they will have a grand Master, they still have the strength to do what they want. As they actively participate in their growth, their souls watch them.

In the future, once they study their beyond lives, they see matters from a new attitude. As a end result, Karma makes it extra hard to start a brand new lifestyles.

This is what the intention is: When the man or woman is ready to take the 5th step, they may be a real Master, and all Karma may be burned up, resolved, and sent back to the supply from in which it came.

Chapter 7: The Best Method for Resolving

Karma

Synopsis

The manner lifestyles is, humans don't continually get what they need. Nobody can trade that. It's possible to consider many exclusive approaches that people's moves affect their lives. One of the most common theories about that is the positivist principle, which says that a person's movements have no effect at all because fate is continually suitable. However, this concept or notion known as Karma says that matters show up for a motive.

Karma takes place whilst a person does some thing top or terrible, regardless of how precise or terrible it is. This is the way it works. This fashionable definition appears to contradict the idea that Karma is always incorrect. There are facets to Karma, the best and the wrong aspect.

Good matters manifest whilst a person does properly things, and terrible matters show up while someone does terrible matters. When you study this, you'll discover ways to keep away from dealing with the results of the alternative. As you understand, mind and feelings are the main matters that make people do what they do. The first-class way to keep away from horrific Karma is to manipulate them. That's why these tips are the first-class matters you may do to save you terrible Karma.

Optimism

More than half of the human beings within the international are called pessimists, which results in things that they do not want or want. So, by means of questioning positively, you may be able to keep away from the results of bad Karma. Trying difficult matters is not clean, however don't give up too speedy. When you do, you give in to the bad power surrounding you. This, in flip, could result in things that might be bad for you and the world.

Failure is the most effective way to grow to be a winner

Too many humans ignore their classes when they fail on the matters they do. Though it can sound crazy, failure is just a step closer to remaining success. Thus, if you keep forgetting about the belongings you do, do not get down about it. Instead, take a look at it as a hazard to take steps to improve your self. You ought to be ready whilst you've been through all the setbacks that someone can think about, says a wise individual. You'll be released to new heights quicker instead of later and must be prepared for that.

The virtue of persistence is a good element to have with you

The value of patience has dropped plenty in latest years, however you continue to want to exercise patience as it enables you learn. It does not paintings that way.

There is continually a time for the whole thing. If you don't learn how to be affected person, you'll emerge as occurring a rampage each time you get into hassle. Now that might be awful Karma, and you don't need to get that awful Karma due to the fact it is able to make your lifestyles horrible.

Chapter 8: Right Relationships End the

Karmic Cycle

Synopsis

The theories of Karma and reincarnation had been tested to be real. They will hold to resolve some of the maximum tough troubles in life. It's some other idea that goes together with the reincarnation concept. It says that there are no injuries or coincidences in existence. Everyone is born into the pre-present conditions of innate dispositions and abilties that they have got discovered over their lives.

Having soul friends and doing appropriate deeds

Many human beings want to know if the man or woman they are with is their soul mate. The concept of soul pals can are available many exceptional bureaucracy, such as whether or not or now not your associate is noticeably romantic, financially profitable, hardworking, satisfaction-orientated, or the toxic one who has a lot of terrible Karma. Some people even are seeking recommendation because they don't recognize that soul mates can are available many different bureaucracy.

Many people have been in complicated relationships. Some human beings had been glad that the connection was over and was hoping they would by no means see their ex once more. Because of your karmic dance, there is a great chance that you may run into humans you do not like, along with commercial enterprise pals, a former lover, or former buddies. This is due to the fact the connection from your previous come upon might not have fully broken down.

Forgive and then let go

There are many methods you will be attracting that man or woman's soul from a destiny lifestyles because you can not let go of bad feelings or emotions for them. Before you die, it's far important that you forgive and be given the way matters turned out. If you don't, you won't be capable of pass on after your loss of life, and also you won't be able to move on after your loss of life.

Be capable of study the equal aspect in another life at some point within the destiny.

Forgiving and studying to allow move is not smooth. Still, it helps you take a look at the bigger photograph and notice a lesson to be remembered after going via hard instances. It also allows you to apprehend different human beings's views and flaws. You can be grateful which you are strong enough to move beyond the harm or pain inflicted on you. A religious, as opposed to spiritual, view of the situation can also help you find the peace you want.

Peaceful Endings stop Karma.

Suppose a dating ends with out a animosity, particularly on your element, and also you simply forgive them. In that case, that indicates that you have the danger to have a good dating with them within the next life if your souls occur to satisfy once more. Likely, your most profitable and near friendships and different relationships on this lifetime were very exclusive from what they had been within the past.

Strong advantageous and bad emotions can be likened to invisible cords that connect souls, making it much more likely that they will meet again inside the future. It's not clean for human beings to get out of karmic debt, specifically in relationships with different human beings. Once someone does so, they are able to reach new heights of personal growth each on a religious stage and on a soul degree.

Chapter 9: Misfortune Always Retribution

For Past Lives

Synopsis

Be capable of analyze the equal element in any other lifestyles in some unspecified time in the future in the destiny.

Forgiving and learning to allow pass isn't smooth. Still, it allows you look at the larger picture and notice a lesson to be remembered after going via difficult instances. It also permits you to apprehend different people's perspectives and flaws. You can be grateful that you are sturdy enough to go past the harm or pain inflicted on you. A religious, in preference to spiritual, view of the scenario may additionally help you discover the peace you need.

Peaceful Endings stop Karma.

Suppose a dating ends without a animosity, specifically on your component, and also you actually forgive them. In that case, that shows which you have the danger to have an amazing courting with them inside the subsequent lifestyles if your souls manifest to fulfill once more. Likely, your most profitable and near friendships and different relationships in this lifetime were very one-of-a-kind from what they have been inside the past.

Strong positive and bad emotions may be likened to invisible cords that connect souls, making it more likely that they will meet again within the destiny. It's not easy for people to get out of karmic debt, specially in relationships with other humans. Once a person does so, they can attain new heights of private boom both on a spiritual level and on a soul degree.

If there simply is a "God", why are there misfortunes and evil?

The answer to this arguable query is indefinite because there are such a lot of motives that may explain why there's and there may be no God. If you try and look at it from a Christian's factor of view, it's far stated that one of these query can in no way be defined because the basis in their belief of the existence of an "Almighty God" is it seems that primarily based on faith. Now you may never query this due to the fact it's miles their manner of life and it is what they saw when they were added into this global.

On the other hand, if you take this question from the factor of view of Buddhists, Pagans and etc, it is however secure to say that they accept as true with otherwise. Others would even say that humans have lived on account that time immemorial however with distinct lives. Though it cannot be denied that ninety nine% of people accept as true with that human beings have constrained time on the earth, it can't be denied that some agree with a lifestyles misplaced is a life won for some other.

Question:

If you consider in reincarnation, is the beyond life determinative of the brand new existence that you are given nowadays?

This is a query that has likewise earned recognition because of the debates and discourses that it brought to the sector. Surely people with exclusive religions will have diverse motives and causes as

regards this question. However, there are many who agree with that Karma is all about retribution – Karma by using the manner is intertwined with the perception of reincarnation.

Karma is in no way approximately retribution due to the fact the factor that it tries to carry to people is the impact of a unmarried or a sequence of acts. It does not usually revolve across the evil international due to the fact if one does excellent deeds, excellent matters will observe. This is quite genuine in a feel due to the fact that is likewise practiced by most Christians – with greater appropriate deeds, God shall shower you with benefits. So it'd be but logical to mention that the beyond lives of people are determinative with the brand new existence they're residing.

In addition to the foregoing, that is in step with the notion of maximum human beings due to the fact with desirable deeds, sufferings and misfortunes might be miles faraway from your lifestyles. Meaning, if you constantly do top for your existence, you'll continually be blessed and be far from getting awful good fortune but in case you do in any other case then horrific good fortune and sufferings will always be to your tail.

LAW OF KARMA

The Vedic religion or so-called Hinduism, there are a few differences from the Abrahamic religions -particularly The Christianity, Judaism, and Islam. The Abrahamic religions do trust in AFTER LIFE – existence after demise. But they do no longer have the concept of Reincarnation. And for Reincarnation to be powerful one needs Law of Karma. These religions do believe in Law of

Karma in ONE or PRESENT lifestyles, however not in carried ahead to FUTURE LIVES. In their idea we're judged on our conduct in ONE existence and there is not a 2nd threat. I also sense that we are able to bypass the Examination if we score greater than 50% on our behavior. But In Vedic idea we may additionally have achieved lots of accurate may be 99 %, we are able to no longer be set FREE from the cycle of Birth and Death till we've got exhausted all the KARMA and their consequences. So, I am writing on this LAW of KARMA and evidently in association with Reincarnation as both pass hand in hand.

In this universe we've got Laws governing the whole thing weather we're aware about it or not. When Sir Isaac Newton saw the apple fall from a tree, he concept of the Reason for the Fruit falling DOWN and not going UP or putting in air and he discovered out the Principle of Gravity after which the Laws that govern the Gravity principle. But the Gravity and the Laws that govern the principle of Gravity existed even before Newton concept about it and came with the standards of Gravity and that they live on even after Newton is long gone. So, we all trust that the whole thing that happens to the gadgets is ruled through some principle or Laws. There are Laws of electromagnetism and lots of different things. We won't understand as to what will take place if we touch live electric twine, however the outcomes will still be there and we are able to have electrical shock. Just because I am not privy to the Laws, does now not suggest that there will no longer be a shock and damage. The Laws exist for big and small – microscopic debris even when we cannot even see them. Even while we talk about Quantum debris and their movement, which has uncertainty, we've got Laws of opportunity that governs the quantum particle movements. So, if there are Laws that control innominate objects, then there need to be some principles that manage our Life and destiny.

When I say The Law of Karma, suddenly every body thinks that that is associated with faith, and one have to have 'faith 'within the faith or GOD and that this isn't scientific Law or principle. But whilst we talk about Law of causation, it sounds clinical, and everybody believes in it. So let me begin by talking approximately the laws that govern our ordinary lifestyles and we've legal guidelines that govern things around us, however we may or won't be aware of the laws that govern them. Everyone has seen apple fall from a tree, however no one knew of gravity or even puzzled as to why the apple falls and now not live hanging in air or can be go UPWARD. It took Newton to consider it after which he got here out with equations that might precisely inform us the gravity and then are expecting precisely the movements of the planets. The identical element befell approximately the Laws that govern electromagnetic subject or thermodynamic laws or planetary motion. So, there are legal guidelines in nature. If I kick a ball, it will journey positive distance. If I kick it more difficult, the ball will journey farther. So, there's purpose -kicking- and impact- ball going farther. So, there may be usually a motive and effect. Even while we DON'T KNOW we try to have relationships in our thoughts. Thunder, hurricanes or storms or seasons and plenty of other matters that humankind is staring at for the reason that humans habituated this earth. When people noticed fever with chills in case of Malaria, we did no longer understand it become caused by Malaria Parasite and spreads with the aid of mosquito chunk. But we knew via commentary that occurrence of so referred to as or named Malaria increases when the AIR IS BAD. So, the name MAL-AIR OR MALERIA. So, there's always cause for everything. So why may want to there be no purpose for our LIFE and things that appear in our lifestyles. All folks have distinctive 'appearance' and mind and lifestyles. We regularly see siblings or siblings who have similar genetics and upbringing, have unique existence. So, one need to try and discover reason for the difference inside the existence. What can be the motive for this sort of distinction. One ought to say it's miles NURTURED or the upbringing or socioeconomic occasions. When we have a look at children at surprisingly early age display fantastic expertise, we name it prodigy. But there have to be a cause a person at relatively early age ought to play an instrument in addition to nicely-educated person musician. The answer that could give an explanation for this stuff is Karmas from Last life and retained reminiscences from preceding existence.

We all know approximately the Action and Reaction. Every Action has Reaction. Sometimes the identical factor is called cause and effect. There is nothing on this observable global, which takes place with out a CAUSE. The Sun rises in East and units in West -has a purpose or purpose -the earth motion across the Sun. There are seasons and there is rain and there are Hurricanes – all have Causes. So why there will no longer be Reaction to Our Action or Karma? So, this is motive and effect regulation. The problem is we recognise this Law and understand -in maximum of the instances and be given it within the whole bodily Universe. But many of us have issue in extending the identical principle to non-bodily universe and then we tend to call those as Luck or Fate and many of us carry in God or resolve to the 'risk' because the cause. Just because we do now not recognize or we can not give an explanation for some thing, does no longer suggest it does not appear. We use fax machines each day. But I do now not assume maximum people KNOW how it works. We see how scientist manage the movement of Voyager tens of millions of miles faraway from us and we do not understand it however be given it as that is SCIENTIFIC! So, the Law of Karma is inside the same category. It is something that we are able to understand it if we examine it. We will communicate approximately the Karma and its results or the relationship and that is the Law of Karma.

Let us start with basic questions -

WHAT IS KARMA OR HOW DO YOU DEFINE KARMA?

IS EVERY 'ACTION' KARMA?

Everybody talks approximately Karma, even folks who do not have any historical past of Hindu philosophy. Whenever someone has terrible issue take place to them, which became either anticipated or sudden, we regularly say, 'That is Karma.' So let us speak approximately this Law of Karma. But before we speak approximately the Law of Karma, we have to define as to what constitutes Karma. Everybody talks about the Karma, and we assume we recognise what Karma is. But whilst we start speakme about it, we've questions. So, we must first define or know as to what Karma is. To define the Karma the best definition can be" any Action is Karma." But that is a simple definition and no longer all Actions might be taken into consideration as the Karma for the reason of this topic. There are sure matters or situations that have to be happy to call it a KARMA for the cause of the Karma with the intention to have results.

So let us study certain ACTIONS and spot how that suits in to our definition.

1 My laptop is likewise doing an action. It allows me to surf the internet. It also shops the statistics or the enter that I installed. It shops my writing, Is it Karma? The vehicle that I drive also has Action, is it Karma? The solution is no and so to name some thing a Karma, IT HAS TO BE DONE BY LIVING BEING. So, the work executed with the aid of system does now not grow to be Karma. Certainly, the matters that I do on computer can be MY ACTIONS and on account that I am a residing entity, as a way to be a Karma and with a purpose to have influence and impact and Reaction. Just to be clear if I send an electronic mail or a hate mail it is going to be an motion or Karma and I can have the Reaction. But now not that of a pc. If I drive a automobile rapid and or carelessly and get in an accident, it's far MY ACTION and not that of my car. So, the work that I do thru a machine is MY ACTION or My Karma and now not the Karma of the device.

SO, TO CONSIDER ANY ACTION AS KARMA, IT MUST BE DONE BY LIVING THING.

2 So, now allow us to talk about our living bodily body. My frame is a residing factor and there are matters going on in my body and I am no longer even privy to them. For example, my stomach secretes acid which enables to digest the food that I devour after which different organs like liver and pancreas and many others. All do secrete the digestive juices and they help digestion. They also cast off toxins or do metabolism of different matters and yes, they do assist or are answerable for the digestion of the food that I consume in addition to the alternative features that these organs do. So, there may be an Action of secretion of the juices and there's a Reaction of digestion of the food, which can be taken into consideration as ACTION - REACTION, So, is it Karma-performed by means of Stomach or Liver and many others.? I have no concept that my belly has secreted acid, or my pancreas is secreting digestive enzyme until I actually have some

disease, so this ACTION of my organs is AUTOMATIC, and I am no longer involved within the procedure. I do not have direct manage over these internal organ feature or their action nor I am aware about the movement. There isn't any DOERSHIP. And so, it isn't always my Karma even though it is achieved in my LIVING BODY.

THERE MUST BE DOERSHIP – FEELING OF I AM DOING IT TO CALL IT KARMA.

3 When the computer is operating or whilst the belly is secreting the acid – do they enjoy or are there feelings of pride or suffering? The laptop isn't always 'glad' or 'sad' as it stored the facts or ship an e mail. The liver isn't satisfied as it got rid of a few pollutants or had digestive juice secreted. The solution is NO, so there's no BHOGTRUTVA- - because of this idea of enjoying or sufferings from the motion, then there's no real KARMA. (BHOG manner playing or disliking) This is mainly essential to take into account as while we keep to do karma and we do now not need

the response to our movement, we need to have the mindset that I neither have desire to experience the matters that provide me delight or keep away from the things – movement that will supply me displeasure. So, this become the 0.33 issue that must be there for any action to be called Karma- the concept of playing the outcomes of the movement or warding off the matters that cause displeasure.

SO, THERE MUST BE BHOGTRUTVA TO CALL IT KARMA AND HAVE EFFECTS.

(I am no longer speakme approximately the act of EATING. The eating is at my discretion and so I DECIDE what to consume when to consume and what kind of to consume and so forth. I pick out the sort of food – the one that offers me nice enjoy. So that is an ACTION. But when the food is offered to the belly – I haven't any ability or manipulate over the in addition method of digestion and so that is not an Action.)

four The tiger catches the deer, kills it, and eats it as this is food for the tiger. Does the tiger have a CHOICE? Can it devour fruits or leaves from a plant? The answer is no. His body isn't always made to devour culmination and he has INSTINCT to kill and eat meat most effective. So, the tiger has no CHOICE. This also is not a real KARMA as there may be no desire. So, to name any motion a Karma there ought to be DOER SHIP(KARTUTVA) WITH CHOICE. (DOERSHIP approach having feeling that 'I' did it) I may also say that there have to be MORAL DIMENSION and FREE WILL to name any movement as Karma.

(The Hindu religion classifies the whole universe in to four classes. These are based on degree of consciousness, and they are one stone degree or nonliving things, is Plant country,three Animal Kingdom and 4 is Human being. The evolution of focus is at highest degree in Human Beings. There is likewise Free Will in Human Being. The mixture of these two things causes the Karma to be finished with Free Will and that causes the Karma or Action to have Fruit or Reaction or influence. In comparison to that the Animal Kingdom is referred to as BHOG YONI, because of this the existence is for hard VASANAS or dreams. So, the animals ACT based totally on Instinct and the goals are not underneath their control. But maximum of the time it's far instinct and now not choice and so they rarely have any Law of Karma applicable for them.)

5.Lastly there should be cosmic effect. If I boost my hand, it is carried out with the aid of me – Living entity, I actually have performed it consciously and Doer deliver (The time period used is KARTUTWA) is there, I know that 'I have done the action' and perhaps it could provide me pride or ache, however there may be no cosmic effect or It does not motive any REACTION and so in genuine sense it is not a KARMA.

We want those five things to be considered to name an movement as a Karma.

It should be performed via Living Thing, it must have DOER SHIP, there have to be BHOGTRUTVA, it need to be performed with CHOICE or Free Will and there ought to be COSMIC EFFECT.

The different truth is that NO ONE may be with out Karma, and all of us must do Karma as long as we're alive. This does encompass such things as bodily functions -voluntary and involuntary, like breathing or heart pumping the blood and other, but additionally easy actions of the body, which might be voluntary.

Now that we realize what a Karma is, the questions begin bobbing up.

There may be such things as

1What changed into the first Karma.

2 Who did the first Karma.

3 What happens to Karma whilst one dies – or bodily frame is destroyed. - which is at the time of demise.

4 How is Karma saved in PRESENT LIFE -whilst we are alive.

five How is Karma carried from one existence to different.

6 Do all of the Karma which might be finished in PRESENT LIFE come to fruition in PRESENT LIFE.

7 If not manifested on this life, then what takes place to them.

eight If we are born with sure Kramas that are going to come back to fruition, then how is the choice achieved (which Karmas are decided on.)

9 What occurs to the Karmas whilst the universe involves quit – the so known as on the time of PRALAY.

10 How to get rid of Karma and their outcomes.

eleven Since we can't STOP doing Karma how can we forestall the Karmas developing outcomes.

I am sure there may be many extra questions and there may be a few questions that one can't have nice answers. But the simple idea will be tried to be clarified in this article.

So, the question is what was the FIRST motion or the Karma and what is taken into consideration as ACTION? One may want to say that the CREATION of the universe is the FIRST Karma.

The query can rise up as to why God might do the KARMA? To do an movement one must have a preference and the desire comes from PAST Experiences and their impressions. (I might now not have preference to fly in aircraft if I have no longer acknowledged or revel in the flying. I could no longer have preference to consume some thing that I have not tasted in past. So, one should have precise experience to ACT) So, to clear up this trouble our religion came out with solution. The Spirit or Purusha, which does now not have any desires because it has no Gunas or qualities, and so has no choice and no impressions, can not produce the Universe. So, one wishes DESIRE to CREATE whatever or do any Karma. The choice comes out of GUNAS. On the alternative hand, the Nature or the PRAKRUTI has no energy and so even though it has Gunas that is the foundation of goals and that can cause action, cannot act because of loss of electricity or spirit, and so it can not produce the universe. So, on the BEGINNING the Purusha and Prakriti or Spirit and Nature get together and bring the Universe. This is what SANKHYA philosophy explains. Again, the Non duality or ADWAITYA believer do not believe in this. But we aren't speakme about it for now. Many have in comparison this to blind and paraplegic getting together to find a manner to move places when one by means of himself cannot do the wanted movement. The blind can't see the course and paraplegic can see however can't walk. But when they get together, the paraplegic sitting at the shoulders of blind can see the direction and manual the blind as to where to go, but blind can stroll however can not see and so can not decide where the right way is to head. So, the mixture will get paintings achieved.

So, how does an man or woman start the First Karma? This is different than the GOD doing first Karma of creation of the universe. If there are no Karmas, there will now not be impressions and if there are not any impressions, how can one have desire which leads to Karma. The answer is tough or impossible. This is just like the question -Did fowl or egg come first in lifestyles. The hen can't pop out without egg and the egg can not come with out a fowl. So, the solution is, there's no proper starting or end. When the Universe ends -and it does, and it does begin once more – all of the living beings merge inside the singularity and that they turn out to be dormant. But the Karma and their impressions do now not go away. So, while the universe is reborn or comes in Active life, the living beings restart their existence with the identical Karma and their effects. We can talk this later. These cycles haven't any starting or the quit and so the question as to

FIRST KARMA, does now not arise or it could be in comparison to the query of which one is first fowl or egg.

So, allow me start with the Karma. The principal principle of Karma is ONE CAN NOT BE WITHOUT THE KARMA AT ANYTIME AS LONG AS ONE IS ALIVE. So, I breath, I devour, I walk or maybe I communicate – a majority of these are Karmas. And they do have response and that is on the spot. So, any action – physical or mental or speech. (क०या -मना -व०चा) is a Karma. So even a notion is an motion. The organs of Action – so referred to as KARMENDRIYAS include speech. So, after I speak- it's miles an action. When I suppose, it is an action and whilst we act bodily, it's far really an action. And every Action has Reaction or in this situation Impression. So, we can also do an motion without a preference initially, however that action will create Impression. AND THERE IS NO WAY TO AVOID IT. So, let us take an example. Someone brings in a special candy that I even have never seen or tasted, and I will don't have any preference. But you then tell me that this is relatively good and wholesome or tastes super and I should attempt it. So, I try it and either I adore it, or I dislike it. Say I adore it. So, I even have properly impact and so next time I am hungry, I will think of this sweet and I will try to have it. When I eat it again, I will have impression and so one can lead to choice to devour and with a view to result in motion and that maintains. This is circle of mind. Repeating the motion leads to intensification of influence and that leads to greater severe preference and that ends in extra motion. This is the precept of any addiction — capsules or alcohol or even smoking.

These impressions are stored in Mind and in Brain. But one may also say that the mind and the brain are long gone when one dies as some distance as physical component is involved. So how can one deliver theses impressions to different Life whilst there may be no physical frame left? The answer is in our philosophy. The Hindu concept is difference. We have 3 our bodies particularly the Causal body, the Astral body and the Physical body or Gross frame (referred to as respectively KARAN SHARIR, SUKSHMA SHARIR AND STHUL SHARIR) These 3 bodies are 'glued' collectively while we're born. The Physical body is what we see and consists of bodily factors and has 5 coverings or sheaths. Thers are Food Sheath or ANNAMAY KOSH, the next one is ENERGY-PRANAMAY KOSH, after which MIND OR MANOMAY KOSHA, THEN THE INTELECT OR DNYANAMAY KOSH AND INSIDE IS ANANDMAYA KOSH or Bliss Sheath. The Astral body has no bodily factors but has MIND-INTELECT – EGO AND CHITTA. The impressions are stored now not most effective in Gross frame or mind however also stored in an Abstract form in Astral body or ASTRAL brain and KARAN SHARIR or CAUSAL BODY (consequently the call CAUSAL frame) But more than just storing them in summary form, they create the Desire to be fulfilled. This brings us in to new lifestyles after the prevailing bodily frame dies. The Causal frame, the Astral Body with its Mind, intellect,

Ego, and Chitta all are nevertheless there after the death of physical body. The handiest element missing is the bodily frame. These dreams cannot be fulfilled with out the bodily body and so we must come returned in new physical frame. If I want to devour sweet, and I don't have any physical body, I can't fulfill my preference to devour the candy and revel in it. So, to enjoy whatever we want bodily frame. We want bodily feel organs to revel in or fulfill our dreams. So, the thoughts and mind may be there after the demise of bodily frame, however with out the physical sense organs one can't fulfill or satisfy the goals.

There is also every other motive we want to be born once more – aside from enjoyable the dreams. If I want to DO GOOD matters - the so known as PUNYA, I need bodily body. When I assist someone, maximum of the times it's miles PHYSICAL HELP. Helping hungry, thirsty, or sick and so on. Providing meals -water drug treatments or safe haven – all are the help to physical body, and one cannot HELP except WE OURSELVES HAVE bodily frame. There are different motives too, just like the debt or GIVE AND TAKE that we have in our bodily existence that creates bondages and attachments and as a way to also need to be repaid or fulfilled. It can be associated with the love and things that we do for it – dating between parents and their children, spouses and friends and lots of other kinds along with expert dating of love and hate. This maintains to create new karmas and attachments and so that it will want to be exhausted earlier than we may be free of these bodies and cycle of Life and Death. But we aren't talking approximately rebirth concept for now.

As I cited above, the impressions are stored Abstract shape. The question might also arise as to what is supposed via 'Abstract shape of garage'? What exactly is abstract shape of impressions? Say I like candy and that influence or preference to consume sweet is saved not for Ice cream or Donuts but simply as liking for sweet. So, when I am reborn, I will like sweet matters which might be to be had in that subculture. So, if I am born in Indian tradition, I will like things like Jalebi or Shree Khand and so on. If I am born in American society, I will love Donut and cakes and tarts etc. So, when new Birth and lifestyles starts, it will have the likes and dislike identical as final existence after which they may be modified as consistent with new impressions and Karmas in gift existence. This is set the Karma and how it creates impressions which in turn creates dreams and the preference have to be fulfilled. That occurs best with physical frame is there and so the rebirth. But I want to speak approximately the Karma and its consequences on our LIFE and FUTURE LIVES.

Now let us observe the consequences of Karma in specific manner. So, as I do any motion physically, I will get the impact of it or so-known as Reaction. The reaction can be instantly or can be later in gift life or can be saved for the reaction to pop out in subsequent lives. One of the commonplace mistakes is that humans sense that every motion or karma can have DIRECT response or impact, and we should be in position to pick out it one after the other. As if there may be a book that tells us what could manifest if I took a pen that did not belong to me or if I would thieve a car what might take place. (In my future lifestyles and unrelated to societal legal guidelines) If I recognize what 'punishment'-Reaction- I am going to get for positive bad action, then I I might think two times earlier than I take that motion. But many a times the Reaction or the outcomes are combination of many Actions and can be difficult to become aware of as one after the other as response to of effect of the authentic Action. So, I took a pen from my office, which did now not belong to me, and I did not pay for it. What would the effect be? One cannot get a solution to this as this movement could have effect, however it'll be mixed with other actions that I have achieved and may not be recognizable because the rection to stealing pen. To classify the Effects of Karma, we need to understand the degrees of Karma. There are 3 types or ranges or tiers of Karma.

1)KRIYAMAN KARMA

2)SANCHIT KARMA

3)PRARABDHA KARMA

1)KRIYAMAN KARMA – As I stated no individual can forestall or live existence with out doing a karma. So, every motion is Karma and the KARMA THAT WE DO IN THIS LIFE IS CALLED KRIYAMAN KARMA. (KRIYA manner ACTION) So, if I breath air – I get oxygen as an effect or impact of Karma of breathing. This is remarkably simple. But we can move one step in advance. If I eat, I get strength is pretty simple to apprehend and all of us do it and expect the result and are not amazed with the effect of our motion or Karma. Next step could be, if I get knowledgeable, visit university, and end up medical doctor, engineer, or accountant, I may have that form of life-style. The accountant can't anticipate to treat patients and the medical doctors isn't expected to do bookkeeping or realize tax legal guidelines. One can not sow seeds for pumpkin and expect orange tree. The outcomes aren't as INSTANTLY seen as taking a breath or ingesting meals. The schooling and revel in and getting a activity and many others. Will need TIME. So, one may also see the effects in few years. But it is nevertheless in this life. Suppose I kicked someone in anger. I might also see the effect proper away – he kicks me. Or if I ran away, the police can also come later, or he may come returned and beat me in few days or months and so forth. Again, there may be time lapsed for the effect to be seen, however it is on this lifestyles. All these things are example of KRIYAMAN KARMA which has effect on this existence. But we've got seen that many a time we see that someone receives away with homicide. Or they beat, threaten, or maybe kill and nothing occurs. The police never capture as they will have no proof or there may be excellent defense or mendacity witness and many others. So, in those cases the KRAYAMAN KARMA does not come to fruition soon or can be not even on this life. But that doesn't suggest that there's no effect of the Karma. The Karma is stored to have effect in destiny existence. So, the stored Karmas are called SANCHIT KARMA. So, some of the Kriyaman Karma gives outcomes immediately and some takes time though nonetheless in this existence and some is saved to show effect in destiny existence – can be next or next to subsequent or so on. But the impact will be there. KRIYAMAN KARMA is the Karma that WE CREAT IN PRESENT LIFE.

2)SANCHIT KARMA – As I said above the Sanchit Karma is saved up Karma. So, we may additionally have executed one million Karmas – in truth, we do lots greater than that, but for sake of debate, say we did a million Karmas. And 100 thousand had their results inside the gift lifestyles and relaxation are left for the effect in subsequent lives. This maintains and so we've a big pot of karmas, and this is referred to as SANCHIT or stored Karmas. This keeps to develop. When we do no longer have any bodily body, we've got little Karma So while our dreams are not fulfilled in ASTRAL world, we decide to come back to physical or Gross global. Depending upon depth of our wants to be fulfilled, we're born to the parents in which they may be fulfilled, and we COME TO THIS WORLD with a part of SANCHIT KARMAS which are going to come to fruition in gift life This pot of Karma which can be going to have the impact in gift life is referred to as PRARABDHA KARMA. So, SANCHIT KARMA are the Karmas that are saved up from SEVERAL LIVES. But best a part of them will come together to return to fruition in ONE LIFE -this is PRARABDHA KARMA.

3)PRARBDHA KARMA -When one is born, she or he can be born with certain Karma that are so called mature now and can be giving the consequences in gift lifestyles. One can also say that they're going to offer fruits to the Karma that one has finished in past lives and had been saved and have not given end result when the Karma turned into performed. The saved Karmas are many and not all can be coming to fruition in ONE life. So, we are born with certain ones that have a risk of giving the consequences in gift surroundings.

(One can effortlessly understand that certain matters have better or less difficult danger of enjoyable in certain surroundings. It can be tough to have American meals in case you are born in African Jungles. Or Indian classical music can not be without problems glad in case you are born in France or Russia. So, the Soul will searching for situations of subsequent life such that the desires will be fulfilled, and the effects of Karma will come to fruitions.)

So, to summarize, we preserve to do Karma and this is Kriyaman Karma and some of them could have consequences on this cutting-edge lifestyles and some could be saved to have results in later lifestyles that is referred to as Sanchit Karma and the Seeds of fruits of Karma which might be going to come back to fruition in PRESENT LIFE, that is predetermined, is referred to as Prarabdha Karma. So, our present lifestyles is decided by using the Karma or matters that we do in this life plus the culmination or the consequences of the Karma that were stored from previous lives -called PRARABDHA.

If I can provide instance of cash, that everybody is aware very without problems, this may grow to be simple. I paintings and make money. Some of the cash that I earn, I spend and a number of the cash that I actually have earned, I will installed bank. I might also spend a number of the cash that I actually have stored in financial institution while the needs get up. But I will no longer be spending all the money that I actually have earned and saved in the bank. I may additionally have a few money given to me via my parents or inheritance. I may want to spend it, or I may keep it in financial institution for future use. So, the money that I earn -is KRIYAMAN KARMA. The inheritance is PRARABDHA KARMA. The cash that I keep in financial institution is SANCHIT KARMA. As possible see from the example, some of the Kriyaman Karma will become Sanchit Karma for destiny lives. Prarabdha Karama is like inheritance – it comes from many preceding lives.

One element to apprehend on this complicated rationalization is that we have a notion that the cycles of birth and dying have continued forever. The cycles of universe coming into lifestyles and the dissolving also are going on for limitless time. So over length of many lives, we've got accrued many extra Karmas than what we do in one lifestyles. So, the pot of SANCHIT KARMA is larger than the pot of KRIYAMAN KARMA – then one which we do in one lifetime. The PRARABDHA is the term used to explain the pot of KARMA THAT WE ARE BORN WITH AND WILL COME TO FRUITION IN PRESENT LIFE. So, that part of our life activities is constant, at least what we will be facing.

We often use terms like Good Luck and Bad Luck. When we get some thing that we can not give an explanation for based totally on our gift Karma, and it's far in IN EXCESS of predicted fulfillment- response then we call it Good Luck. When we get response that is LESS THAN what we predicted or can give an explanation for based on our know-how of our efforts or situation, we name it BAD LUCK. The UNKNOWN aspect that changes the final results, both for higher or worse is because of PRARABDH KARMA or the Karma that we're born with and are GOING TO COME TO FRUITUION weather we love it or no longer, climate we realize about it or now not. Another element that also can alternate the outcome is FREE WILL.

We additionally talk about PUNYA and PAP. The Karmas which are ethical or right, will have consequences that are properly, and we call it PUNYA. The Karmas that are immoral or bad will cause detrimental results and we name that as PAP. When we do new Karmas in gift life, they're also labeled as suitable and terrible, and they'll upload to either gift life results or can be stored for destiny life outcomes. So once in a while we see God Loving ethical individuals who go through, and criminals seem to escape the punishment on this existence. This may be explained primarily based on Prarabdh Karma and Kriyaman Karma being specific

KRIYAMAN KARMA------------------------------------
------------------------------------PRARABDH
KARAM

(FROM ACTIONS IN PRESENT LIFE) (GOING TO
COME TO FRUITION IN PRESENT LIFE)

Relationship between the three styles of
Karma is there. Sanchit Krama is TOTAL
STORED KARMA, but the KRIYAMAN Karma –
can add to it. The Prarbdha Karma is FIXED
but the Kriayaman Karma can upload to it too.

Let us see what distinctive KARMAS are. It
changed into said that we are able to act with
bodily frame -Act with Mind – Act with the
Speech. Each is exceptional in its effect or
Impression or response that may occur when
best mind or speech engages in doing Karma.
Certainly, or all 3 can combine and then the
impact is greater severe.

Everybody has clean expertise of Physical
Karma. I stroll or I write, or I consume – a lot
of these bodily sports are smooth to
understand as Karma and clean to see the

71

results. If I do whatever physically it will have effects. But If I even have ONLY terrible thoughts about a person, and I actually have now not taken any movement, am I still doing Karma? If I think that someone should not get a process or fail in exam etc., am I doing Karma? Or for that if I even have precise thoughts, I am doing a Karma? The answer is YES. The Karma is not best bodily however additionally mental and the intellectual is as essential as physical. The Physical Karma is visible but Mental Karma isn't always seen but has impact. But the notion method need to be sustained and frequent to have a great deal extra and deeper Impressions after which the outcomes. If I see someone stealing cash or beating a person, and I even have a thought that that individual need to be stuck and punished, there is a Karma and in an effort to have response, however it is weak. I have no longer performed equal thinking all the time. But if I continue to have same concept again and again — lust for someone or wondering bad destiny for a person, so as to have results can be not in this life. But it'll be stored and in destiny life or destiny lives we are able to have hatred or love for that same man or woman. All of us have experienced like or dislike or maybe hatred in the direction of some individual that we have in no way met. We all have experience this in our lifestyles that we like a person for no obvious purpose. So, severe, repeated thought-although now not followed with the aid of physical action, will have consequences on long time. Again, a informal idea of dislike or like does not purpose an awful lot response that's durable and genuinely now not carried to subsequent life.

Let us talk approximately the Physical Action or Karma. As become cited, the physical motion does constitute Karma in most of the instances however not all. So many thoughts won't reason lasting response or impression, however a few do. Exactly opposite is real with Physical Action or Karma. Many or maximum bodily Karma will cause affect and Reaction. So now the query comes if I do physical interest and don't have any intellectual concept at the back of it, could I actually have same effects as simply doing bodily movement. The solution is little complicated. Suppose I am on foot, and I overwhelmed a roach, and I am not aware of it, did I do the karma? And if I overwhelmed roach with intention of killing the roach, did I do one-of-a-kind Karma? The final results is same, in both instances which is- 'I KILLED A ROACH' 'The intellectual idea in the back of every physical motion is in particular crucial. I were given mad at someone and kicked him, and I was taking walks and appear to kick someone by means of mistake without any intension of kicking -is there a difference inside the Reaction which can occur to the motion? And to add to that say I express regret, and I make an apology. The consequences of Karma with out a idea of kicking, may have honestly little outcomes. Take an instance of praying God. If I pray God for purchasing favors for MYSELF-money-energy etc., it's far distinctive than if I pray God to have horrible matters show up to someone that I do not like and lastly, I pray

God with just love and ask for no favors for myself -no call for to get something in go back. In all cases I am asking God for a favor. But the effect of these Karmas could be extraordinary. The last one is Sattvic Guna prayer and the only wherein we are asking some thing for our self is Rajasic Guna prayer and the one in which we're asking God to have horrible things manifest to someone is Tamasic. The outcomes of theses KARMA may be one-of-a-kind though the PHISICAL Action become the same. So, the mental idea process is important or purpose behind the physical motion is specially vital and determines the REACTION or culmination of our motion or Karma. In case of Prayer to God for his Love and no fabric benefit has no bondage or Karma. But the reaction to the movement of prayer for asking to hurt a person will be bad and one for the favors for oneself might be to get in extra attachments and bondage. So now you may recognize how the same Karma may have one-of-a-kind consequences.

Let me supply another instance. There turned into this man sitting doing or trying meditation. A fearful man ran beyond with the aid of him and informed him no longer to inform which path he went as some terrible guys had been looking to kill him and were after him. In short time a few men with knifes drawn came and requested him if he saw a man going for walks and if he did, which course he went. The person who became meditating knew that telling a lie is not accurate and so he stated yes and pointed to the route the man had long past. So, did he do the good Karma or the bad Karma and what type of effect will that have. In one case even though he advised the truth – which is meant to be a Good Karma the impact of telling the reality prompted a person harm and in order that isn't always an excellent Karma and telling a lie is bad in maximum cases, however in this case, he saved someone's life with the aid of telling a lie that makes it a great Karma. So now we understand the effects of Karma as to how they might be specific for identical Karma, and one can be amazed. But one ought to use commonplace feel.

Now the query arises as to why some individuals who continue to do horrific moves- Karma throughout their whole existence that we have recognized, do now not seem to have bad final results, but have splendid lifestyles. They appear to 'break out' any reaction or punishment for his or her terrible movement. The answer is in what I stated above as to the distinction in 3 sorts of Karma. The terrible deeds that they may be engaged in is Kriyaman Karma and it may or may not have consequences straight away or inside the same life. So, the horrific deeds or Karma can have bad final results for certain, however it can be next or subsequent to subsequent life. Not all the stored Karma or Sanchit Karma will come to fruition in next lifestyles. Some will come faster to fruition, and a few will show impact in next-to-subsequent life or may be after 5 lives.

I can supply some of the examples in realistic existence which can explain this. We have visible in our bathe a knob which could adjust warm and cold water. When we need to get warm water, we turn the knob to Hot water side and then as the new water begins, we flip the knob to less warm facet, the water glide remains warm, and it takes time before the water turns into cooler. So, the impact of turning knob isn't always immediately however takes time. Something similar can be seen with Good and Bad Karma. Even while we've completed Good Karma the impact isn't always on the spot. And when we have executed Bad Karma, the impact isn't always visible right away. Another example that is like this is example of the cereal dispenser in resorts wherein the dispenser is stuffed from the top and the cereals are dispensed from backside in which you may get as tons as you need. Suppose you've got cereal dispenser packed with corn flakes after which as humans get corn flakes out of the dispenser, it starts offevolved getting low. So, you fill it with fruit loops. Now when you try to get cereals from the bottom, you will preserve to get corn flakes until the dispenser has corn flakes and as the corn flakes run out you will start getting fruit loops. There may be a brief time when you get both -the corn flakes and fruit loops combined collectively whilst you turn the knob on the dispenser, The Karma that we do aren't organized one on pinnacle of different, like cereal dispenser- one type like corn flakes or fruit loops and many others. But they're of numerous kinds with distinctive response -degree in addition to sorts – accurate or bad. Moreover, they're no longer stored one at the pinnacle of other. They aren't stacked as though older Karma could have results earlier than the newer Karma. So, we may additionally see the outcomes of older Karmas subsequently or may additionally take many lives. This has to do with what kind of life one 'Selects' and if the results or fruits of Karma has a chance to materialized or come to fruition in that lifestyles. It is not like older Karma can have results in advance than recent Karma. To state it any other way – there's no fixed

Incubation Period earlier than the results or the reaction to Karma manifests. They will all have outcomes or come to fruition however no longer the way in collection they were performed. The intensity of out goals and depth of our studies from the Karma will manual whilst and how they come to fruition. So, one may have preference for song and may have done a few schooling in track and that could convey her or him to be born to musician dad and mom. But he may additionally have alcoholism and so that may be different desire and attachment. But he may also have love for the father or mom from preceding existence. So, those 3 desires will want to be fulfilled. But the intensity of each may be extraordinary and when the soul desires to be born, the situation won't be conducive to satisfy all the dreams at one time. So, all can't be coming to fruition in a single lifestyles. So, there are a couple of elements which are available in play when one is born and so positive Karmas that have risk to come to fruition are sure collectively and this is referred to as Prarabdh.So, in the above example of cereals dispenser there is one difference. The dispenser has handiest one sort of cereal coming out at a given time. Not so for outcomes of Karmas. There are lots of Karmas that we do in our ONE lifestyles, and we've numerous hundreds of lives. The reaction to theses Karmas is waiting to be fulfilled and the impact isn't one after the other, but the outcome is very last effects of many similar Karmas -so known as COMBINED EFFECT. If we see some results or see the sufferings or happiness in someone's existence it's miles impossible to understand as to which Karma induced that impact. So, it's miles hard to study something and try and parent out as to what need to be the Karma that brought about the effect. This has to do with the truth that the effects are aggregate of all the pulls or the effects of many reactions. Let us take an instance of a stone. We connect a rope to it and pull it. The stone will move in one route. The path might be determined by way of the route of the force and the power of the pull or force. So, if the pressure is robust, then the movement could be brief, and the path will be in most effective one route – the route is decided by using the course of the pull. But like tug of warfare, if there are two pulls the motion can be decided by using the more potent of the forces or the ensuing force and the course may also be determined by means of the more potent force. It is likewise viable that the path may additionally exchange if the pressure on one facet becomes weaker or stronger with passing time. So, the direction will be changed, and the rate of motion also may be quicker or slower relying upon the power of the pressure. This is quite easy to apprehend. But now consider no longer one, no longer but many- can be one hundred or a thousand of forces pulling OUR LIFE in many unique directions. The forces have different path and power and may exchange with time. Add to that our FREE WILL. The life might be determined by means of RESULTANT of these types of forces. It may be impossible to find out as to which Karma brought on which reaction or effect and which direction the existence if going.

In quick if we have one to one impact – ACTION AND REACTION TO THE KARMA- then it'll be extremely smooth to look. Which action brought about what effect. But here we are seeing more than one pulls on our lifestyles as an impact of more than one Karmas coming to fruition. So, the ensuing course may be determined based on the force or depth of the effects of Karma. There is one greater pressure that could upload additional force that could change the direction. So, a few human beings name this as ADRUSHYA KARMA- one that can not be visible. This is FREE WILL. But even before the FREE WILL, we should recognize how these 'stored karma' exchange the direction of our present motion or karma. Someone had stated that there are 4 viable effects of our present Action or Karma. We act for particular effect, and we get it -this is one and simple to recognize. Then we Act and get MORE effect that we expected -this is 2d. We Act and ger LESS than we expected -this is 0.33 and ultimately, we Act and get VERY DIFFERENT impact than we predicted not extra, now not much less but one-of-a-kind impact. Why would this happen? The answer is within the PRARABDH Karma – the Karma that we are born with to have come to FRUITION IN THIS PRESENT LIFE. We are not aware about what effects these Karma are going to have or when they're going to have or how robust the effects are going to be. But this is the game changer. So, that is the referred to as ADRUSHYA or UNSEEN, UNEXPECTED FORCE that alters the end result of our gift lifestyles Karma. I will deliver an instance. You need to go somewhere, or paintings and also you need to seize a bus. You are waiting for the bus. So, there are four possibilities of what can happen. One is that the bus comes in on time and you visit paintings as you wanted. So, your movement had same response. Second opportunity is that bus comes overdue or does now not come in any respect, and also you pass over going to paintings. So, this time your motion gave you poor reaction or opposite response. The 0.33 possibility is that your friend shows up at the same time as you are ready and gives you lift and drops you to work in his automobile. This is more than what you predicted. And fourth possibility is that during seeking to get in the bus, you fall and wreck your leg. So, in this example, to procure 4 one-of-a-kind responses. One became matching achievement, different was matching failure, and 0.33 became more achievement than what you predicted and closing became distinct and worse than you expected. In existence we've got distinct responses to out motion and the forces that CHANGE the response are due to hidden forces of PRARABDH KARMA- the Karmas that we are born with from previous lives and are going to return to fruition inside the gift existence. We do not understand them, and we do not realize as to what become the original karma that caused the response or the amplitude of the hidden reaction. If we knew, then maybe we ought to attempt to trade the path. One may want to have started out in advance so we do now not pass over the bus, or you will be careful and no longer fall. But you do not recognize and so you have trouble in warding off the pressure which could exchange the reaction.

Many human beings query the life of Free will. Many trust that there may be no Free Will, and the Destiny is predetermined and that isn't going to alternate. The lifestyles that we are going to have been predetermined and we have "no say" or function within the dedication of our very own life or which course it's going to cross. I have some clarification. So, become the FIRST LIFE determined by means of FREE WILL as there was no preceding lifestyles to decide? If we begin going again many lives, we can hold to have equal question as to what caused the future lifestyles. So, we are able to cross on going again and returned may be 10000 lives and we will have identical query and identical solutions. So, I cannot solution as HOW THE FIRST LIFE DIRECTION WAS DETERMINED? If there were no previous Karma, then there was no choice and there were no moves to go away any impression or Karma that might come to fruition. So how was first life decided. This is once more just like the question as to which got here first – hen or the egg. The egg comes from hen and bird comes from the egg. One can not have fowl without egg and the same manner the Destiny can not pop out of not anything and if there has been no Karma to decide the next existence how changed into the primary existence decided.

In Hindu thinking there's no beginning or cease to the cycles of universe being born or finishing. This cycle maintains and it has no beginning or give up, and the Karmas are carried from one life to different and one cycle to different and so there's no question of whilst the first lifestyles become as there may be no first lifestyles.

So, let me attempt to give an explanation for the predetermined existence and Free will. Our entire crook and moral structures are based on assumption that we've got FREE WILL. When one commits a criminal offense – stealing or beating or killing someone, we

BELIEVE that he did it with FREE WILL and he had a CHOICE now not to do it. He did the act with Free will and NOONE FORCED him to do it. The insanity protection that we see in a few instances argues that there has been no unfastened will and so that is carried out simplest in some instances. But how a good deal FREE is FREE WILL is the query. Based on what I actually have said we are born with sure Karmas that are going to come back to fruition in present lifestyles. But we additionally do extra Karma and with a purpose to upload to the consequences on this existence and some in future lives. Our present life is determined by means of the Karmas which are going to come back to fruition on this existence -that we're born with and the addition of the Karmas that we're DOING in gift lifestyles and are going to have effects in gift lifestyles. (To make it easy a person may additionally have diabetes if you want to have an effect on the blood sugar with a purpose to be higher than everyday. That is what he's born with or has it as the Karmic effect. Then he eats candies and with a purpose to make blood sugar worse -or takes medicines and adjustments weight-reduction plan so that it will lessen the blood sugar – Actions or Karma that he's doing in present lifestyles -both these ACTIONS and Karmas will have blended effect.) So, the occasions which are going to are available in our lifestyles WILL HAPPEN, however how we REACT to it's miles in our hands. A character has diabetes is from his Karma the PRARABDHA Karma that he is born with (and being born to diabetic mother and father is also results of Karma) and that can't be changed. How he reacts to devour – through taking drug treatments and following diet and exercising etc. Is his KRIYAMAN Karma or Karma from gift lifestyles. The resultant may be decided through HIS BEHAVIOUR and the severity of his diabetes. The formerly stored Karma and their outcomes that are going to come back to fruition in this life, could have a force and many of us may not have enough desire, electricity, or time to fight it. But we do have free will. If we did now not have unfastened will, we can not be held answerable for our movements or Karmas. Someone may additionally say that if we act in step with dreams and attachments and the Karmas from past, then where is free will? To some quantity the so-referred to as Destiny is FIXED when we are born. When a diabetic WANTS to devour more sugar as he loves sweet things, that is because of beyond lifestyles reports and Karmas and impressions saved from them and coming to fruition in present life. Some also will declare that the whole thing is motive and impact. The Sun rises in east and sets in west is because of a reason. The seasons that we see have reason or cause after which seasons are the impact. Kamic outcomes of the Karma which are going to return to fruition is fixed and so, that a part of Destiny is fixed and predetermined. But now not the entire life. What I imply by way of this assertion is that the events which are going to occur in our life is predetermined primarily based on the results or the response to the Action or Karma that we've finished in beyond lives, and they're coming to fruition in the gift life. So, what is PREDEERMINED is which Karma consequences are going to have their results on our gift existence. So, in that experience the destiny is predetermined on the time of start. I actually have some concept at the evidence or so-referred to as medical thought technique on this primarily based on some observations of recent borne babies. Consider our existence as 4 lane dual carriageway. (Or can be 10 or 20 lanes) The route, the speed, and the lane that we're using is PREDETERMINED via the previous Karmas, but it is in our arms to sluggish down or move faster or exchange lane or maybe take exit and from time to time trade course. This is unfastened will. But we can need to combat difficult or tougher to alternate the course. Sometimes little efforts are wanted and every now and then we have to do lots of efforts. And from time to time we definitely can't do it even when we strive. So, there are three various things that may show up. One is that the results of preceding Karma can be nullified by means of minor attempt, 2nd, the consequences of previous Karma may be nullified by using masses of efforts after which thirdly there's no way to nullify effect of positive Karmas from preceding existence.

If I raise my hand virtually no one can say that there was no free will. I might also enhance my hand, or I might not. And on the grounds that I RAISED MY HAND without a person telling me to raise the hand, I have to have loose will to raise my hand. There are a few those who feel that there's no FREE WILL and there are experiments showing that before we FEEL we've got decided, there are reactions in mind recorder via EEG. So, whilst the mind electric pastime become recorded, it preceded the concept. The individual became asked to inform while he become going to raise the hand. The electrical interest preceded the concept. (This test from 1980, performed by way of Bejamin Libet is frequently quoted. The one that was performed and said in 2021 debunked the idea of Libet that we do no longer have unfastened will.) But is that because of KARMA or is there a unfastened will and with the Free Will we determined to elevate the

92

hand? But I sense that metaphorically speakme, the DESIRE to raise the hand comes from previous Karmas and weather to elevate or not is OUR selection. This is quite easy instance and that could look absurd- why might Karma make me raise the hand-in essence the elevating hand isn't a true Karma until it is executed to reply a question in a category or to hit someone and many others. But this is simply as an example. In Hindu theology there are four LANGUAGES. They are referred to as PARA-PASHYANTI - MADHYAMA-VAIKHARI. The Vaikhari is the spoken language but before whatever turns into 'spoken notion,' it ought to have an origin. This chain of origin of notion is the one of a kind languages. PARA may be considered as a small wave inside the ocean of our MIND after which we VISUALISED the notion-that is PASHYANTI, then there is a hyperlink, earlier than the idea will become spoken words -this is referred to as MADHYAMA. So, in this whole technique the bodily mind reacts simplest while the decision is made to verbalize or take a few motion the EEG may have preceded the real action. So, I am not surprised that there's a few brain pastime earlier than the real physical movement.

Let us communicate about the Free Will in a practical existence as opposed to the in-lab experiment. Why in a few cases we sense that there is no unfastened will, or the loose will does no longer work. (Remember what I stated earlier than -not every impact of Past Karma may be neutralized -a few may be carried out with little efforts, some with plenty of efforts and a few CANNOT be nullified.) Let me give an explanation for with couple of examples which might be given by means of others and there can be many other comparable examples. Say we have a yellow coloration wall, and we want to make it or paint it blue. So, to paint it blue, we want paint, brush, goals, and time and many others. So, if I begin portray the wall and I deliver one coat, then the wall will not be Blue, however it is going to be green- yellow plus blue is inexperienced. So, if I do not have enough paint or desire or materials or time, then the wall will not be Blue, however it is going to be yellow or inexperienced. So, the final results or the product is dependent upon many elements which are associated with OUR FREE WILL. The yellow wall represents the PRARBDHA KARMA which might be going to return to fruition, and we are able to stay with yellow wall or alternate it depending upon our desire and efforts and availability of materials. In positive situations, we can also have one or two but now not all the matters that are needed to alternate the coloration or the culmination of the beyond Karmas.

Let us take any other example. We have exam tomorrow and we've no longer studied for complete 12 months. The outcome is constant – we are able to fail the instance. This is PRARABDHA – the Karmas that are going to return to fruition. The state of affairs that we will now not take a look at till the exam, is PREDETERMINED and we had FREE WILL to alternate it while we joined the magnificence. So, to study in time we have unfastened will and desire and we could study and CHANGE the final results or the culmination of our previous karmas. But maximum folks will no longer do it.

In practical life we regularly see FREE will. We are in someone's home and there may be meals for celebration to be served. We do no longer snatch the food until the host tells us to take it. We do no longer urinate in public. We can be mad at a person, but we do no longer beat them. We use FREE will all of the time.

Some people will name matters that can not be modified as Destini.

So, allow us to take every other example, we are in motorboat and the boat has some velocity and the current of the river has a few pace. So modern-day will be in the identical course because the course of our boat or might be contrary in route. Let us say it's miles in the identical direction and it is twenty miles according to hour and the rate of the motorboat thirty miles. We can be moving within the route of our destination at the speed of 20 +30 = 50 miles according to hour. So, we are shifting toward our goal at an awful lot faster than our boat.(This is in comparison to the reaction or reward to our Karma being MORE THAN our efforts or expectation as cited above because of the assist from the rewards that we've coming to fruitions from the Karma that we did in previous lifestyles and are coming to fruition in this existence) So, the velocity of river current is our PRARABDHA or results of Karma that are coming to fruition. And adding to that is our choice and efforts to get to the intention and we are able to be successful QUICKER. So, we name this as GOOD LUCK OR GOOD FORTUNE. But let us say that the contemporary of the river water is twenty miles additionally however in contrary direction than we want to go, and we've motorboat, and we are transferring at velocity of twenty miles. You recognise what is going to manifest to us as a long way as transferring towards aim. We could be stagnated, and we recognise how we do experience now and again in lifestyles. But we've a motorboat, and we are able to increase the velocity and what kind of we can boom the velocity is up to our efforts and what sort of motorboat we have. (The form of motorboat that we've is based on out Previous Karma) But if we can trade the speed and go at pace of 30 miles, we are able to flow toward our purpose at simplest 10 miles,30-20 =10. So, in this example while our preceding Karma aren't favoring our movements to get to our intention, we can circulate slower, however we are able to pass and again this is our FREE WILL. (This falls underneath the category of LESS THAN EXPECTED rewards for our gift Life Karma)

(Brief observe on Indian Astrology and the future and Free Will. The natal chart-the Horoscope that astrologer prepares primarily based on the time of delivery and the location of birth is the recommendations for the THINGS to COME. In quick, the location of the planets tells us what type of life we can have or in brief, the PRARABDHA – the Karmas that are going to come to fruition. So, this has near relation with the word Destiny and the predetermined course that we're going to must stroll. But that does not suggest that we can't exchange. This is the purpose now not all predictions are accurate or correct. Certainly, Free Will has something to do with it too. The prediction based totally on gross natal chart is not going to be 100% ideal, but there may be other manner to expect which includes Nakshtra role and Dasha and Mahadasha of various planets and some thing known as Nawamaunsh Kundali and ultimately Intuition of the person who is reading it. I do no longer recognise an awful lot to touch upon natal chart, however just to say speedy the Indian or Vedic astrology is primarily based on role of Moon and so it adjustments every 2.33 days and Nakshtra are twenty-seven exceptional constellations obvious from the earth that also assist divide people born on comparable dates – time however now not exact time. So, the planetary function is the PRARABDHA and that may be changed to a degree by way of Free Will. The Sun seems to skip thru the twelve zodiac signs and symptoms in three hundred and sixty five days and so it remains in every signal for one month -more or less. This is the Zodiac sign up western astrology. But in Eastern Astrology the signal is based totally on position of moon and that changes each 2.33 days kind of and in order that differentiate people in separate groups more after which when you speak approximately in addition division through NALSHATRs which are7 we have a good deal more correct division and may be prediction)

In Hindu Religion we do no longer have time period for Free Will. But we communicate approximately PURUSHARTH.A simple meaning of the word Purusharth, is anything is carried out by Human Being or the obligations of the Human Beings. The scripture divides the Purusharth in 4 distinct kinds, specifically

1DHARM

2ARTHA

3KAMA

four MOKSHA.

The Dharma way faith in this context. Artha way Money, Kama manner pleasurable goals and Moksha way freedom from cycle of beginning and loss of life. We are speculated to do efforts for these 4 various things. One need to behave in RIGHT or Religious manner, Dharma, to make Money-ARTH, and fulfill our Desires – KAMA and on the give up attain Moksha or Nirvana or freedom. As you'll be able to see of these 4 are to a point predetermined with the aid of Prarabdha -by means of the Karma that we've got done in beyond lives and are going to come back to fruition. These are ARTH and KAMA. As I referred to climate, we are going to have lots of cash or now not is predetermined to a few expand and despite the fact that that can be modified by means of our efforts in gift stay, that part is limited. The identical holds genuine of which goals are going to be fulfilled in present lifestyles, which is KAMA.

(WE ARE BORN TO FULFILL OUR DESIRES ANYWAY) The efforts to BEHAVE in proper or non secular manner is in our arms and to paintings to get closer to Moksha is also in our arms. But maximum of us work harder to get extra cash and have our dreams glad. So, to paintings on these things is Free Will or Purusharth consistent with Hindu Religion. This does no longer imply that one must now not do any efforts to make cash or satisfy goals. But it sincerely manner that we're born with positive barriers. One have to make every attempt to alternate it for higher, but at the same time be given the outcome as to a point it is predetermined. Unless we do the efforts, we will no longer know what is predetermined. So as is stated in Geeta, to do efforts or Action or Karma is in our palms - now not the end result of it. The end result can be there and regardless of the fruit is we have to accept it. (This Shloka is defined latter.)

The Karma also may be divided in to 3 awesome categories

1 SAKARMA -The Karma this is prescribed via our religion or morality

2 VIKARMA – The Karma that is to be averted

three AKARMA The Karma that does not cause reaction.

The SAKARMA is a Good Karma suggested and the morally right and that reasons PUNYA or positive reaction. This might be on the spot or delayed as noted above.

The VIKARMA is the one which should be avoided like stealing, killing mendacity and so on. And that causes PAP. Again, reaction or the fruit can be immediately or not on time as cited above.

The AKARMA is the Karma, which does no longer CREATE any response or has fruit as it's far achieved without any expectation of end result.

SLEEP AND REINCARNATION?

Now a quick notice on what I said on the so called my evidence for how we are borne with sure Karmas that are going to come to fruition on this lifestyles. This is based on looking the sleep pattern. Every animal ought to sleep and there is a restoration of the brain and other organs at some point of the sleep. Without the sleep all of the dwelling matters will die. There are modifications in secretions of many hormones that have diurnal cycle and without sleep there will be problem with fitness. During sleep there is consolidation of memory that occurs at some stage in sleep. There are awesome sorts of memories- so-called LONG-TERM MEMORY. There is Declarative or Explicit memory. This is like learning different things and bringing it lower back while asked for. Declarative memory is divided into Episodic memory, Semantic reminiscence, Spatial reminiscence, and ultimately Autobiographical memory. In contrast to that the Procedural memory has Perceptual Learning, Category Learning, Emotional Learning and ultimately Procedural Learning. Procedural studying is done from previous reports and that consists of simple such things as tying shoelaces to motorbike driving and playing a few musical device. This takes place on the unconscious stage.

We have wonderful ranges of sleep. The sleep is divided in numerous tiers based on the electrical interest of the mind. The sleep is divided into NON-REM SLEEP and REM SLEEP. So, there may be a stage called REM – Rapid Eye Movement sleep. In this stage the eyes flow rapidly and so it is referred to as REM or Rapid Eye Movement sleep. Majority of the dreams take place in this level of the sleep and maximum of the REM degree happens in 2nd half of of the sleep. The dreams in this degree of sleep are complicated and do not seem to be structured upon external stimuli The other levels of sleep are known as NON-REM sleep. In Non-REM sleep there's Stage one that is light degree of sleep, then there is stage 2 sleep and stage 3 and 4. Now a days blended to call SLOW WAVE SLEEP or SWS. The brain wave hobby shows sluggish wave and so it's far referred to as slow wave sleep and it is the private of the sleep stages. The goals that occur in non-REM sleep are simple and REM sleep dreams are complex. The percentage of each level of sleep is exclusive in one of a kind age agencies. As an grownup we have level 2 sleep contributing nearly 50 % of the total sleep and the REM is 20-25 % and SWS is also 20 %. In REM sleep we CONSOLIDATE reminiscence – (Procedural and emotional memory) at least one kind of memory. In adult life we've got stage 1 sleep after which other levels of sleep now not necessarily within the order of numbers, but the SWS takes place in first 1/2 of night extra than in second half and the REM sleep takes place extra in 2nd half of of the night than first half of. But in Newborn little one the SLEEP Starts with REM SLEEP. This happens in first in three months of lifestyles while newborn toddler sleeps for 18 hours an afternoon. The little one cannot focus thoroughly -eyesight isn't always mature sufficient at that time. So, the question that I actually have is what sort of MEMORY CONSOLIDATION the new child infant is doing that desires 50 % of the sleep that's REM? The pastime that the toddler at this age of existence is so confined that there isn't always lots reminiscence to be consolidated. This memory is Procedural and emotional reminiscence. So why does it have extra REM sleep than adult. There is extra want for consolidation of the memory – just like the jobs and names of various human beings that we meet and research that we need to do as scholar and roads and plenty of other activities like riding and games that we play and so on.(SWS is very crucial for such different reminiscence and has exceptional brain centers, and could be very essential in grownup existence) So, what's it that the brand new borne infant is consolidating in first three months of life that it desires extra of REM sleep? My feeling or rationalization is that the new child infant is CONSOLIDATING MEMORY FROM LAST LIFE in an abstract shape. The karmic consequences which might be stored in Abstract shape after loss of life of bodily frame from ultimate lives, and which might be now going to return to fruition on this life -need to be consolidated. And that part is occurring in first 3 months or so. The infant which has not lots exposure to surroundings in average day of 24 hours, in which it sleeps for 18 hours. So, why does it want greater REM sleep. (Not to consolidate memory from gift life however to consolidate recollections from final lives.) This can be taken into consideration as moving antique data from your vintage phone or antique computer to new smartphone or computer. (The pc may be compared to our human body. The CPU is bodily brain, and the hard pressure is like Astral frame or Subtle frame. STHUL SHARIR or the brain in bodily body need to have those reminiscences.

The second form of reminiscence consolidation that occurs in REM sleep is emotional reminiscence. We are uncovered to many stuff that create emotion and people memory are consolidated. If we see a few photographs which can be gross or witness an coincidence where a person changed into injured or killed or have a few enjoy of Love, a lot of these are emotional recollections, and they're 'consolidated' in memory. So, what kind of EMOTIONAL MEMORY a newborn infant could have throughout the daily existence. As all of us recognise that the new child little one spends maximum of the time in sleep and relaxation in drinking milk /components, pooping, urinating, and getting changed. It does have a touch with mother and father and a few other household but the imaginative and prescient is not ordinary and so I am now not positive there are numerous EMOTIONAL MEMORIES that I can think of in the course of that time. So, what emotional memories it'd consolidate? COULD IT BE SOME FROM PREVIOUS LIVES that it is wearing to be popping out on this lifestyles and could have an effect on the persona in gift lifestyles? Predominant REM sleep which is likewise known as Active Sleep seen in early infancy is in any other case hard to provide an explanation for. SWS -gradual wave sleep also consolidate certain memories as cited above, but they are from PRESENT LIFE and so that is less at early infancy and then will increase as we emerge as grownup. So, on the grounds that we do no longer have a good deal studying done for first few months of existence, we've got much less of SWS. Please notice that this natural hypothesis on my component and there's no medical or scientific proof.

While we're on the topic of goals and sleep, we've regularly skilled the dreams wherein we see matters that we've got never seen or experienced in Present existence. How can one see matters in desires that we've got by no means seen? The solution can be that we might not have seen those matters – places, surroundings in Present lifestyles, however we may have visible or experienced them in preceding lives, and they come to surface - stored from ultimate lives! Again, that is natural hypothesis on my part and there may be no proof for this announcement.

LAW OF KARMA AND REINCARNATION

When we communicate approximately Karma and its results on our life, we also are speaking approximately the opposite Principle -the reincarnation. So, the Law of Karma goes hand in hand with the reincarnation. The Karma and its consequences on us and the impressions that it generates causes the rebirth. When we interact in any Action or Karma, we now not most effective have a few Reaction or impact related to our action, but we additionally set in movement something else. While we do an motion, we also have a few Give- and take or debt that we create. We also get a few attachment. Let us take an instance. I will use vintage examples and add a few new ones to make this point clear. I like chocolate. So, once I eat it, I get delight -the affect of ingesting the chocolate and that causes more choice to devour greater chocolate. But this is an attachment to chocolate. If a person gave me the chocolate, then I even have a debt from that someone who glad my Desire. So, we've an attachment, we have advent of Desire, and we've got an Attachment. This is on material factor, however then there's attachment related to emotions. We have emotional attachment with our families — mother and father, siblings, spouses, pals, and friends and so on.

The emotional attachments are also robust attachments – may be even more intense than one with bodily matters. So, there are Effects of Karma that should be resolved and there are debts that must be repaid. I may additionally have helped someone with food, refuge, water, or cash. That should be repaid in some shape. The same issue on our emotional levels. This will convey us lower back to the environment in which these things can be fulfilled. The bonds of affection and relationships and for that matter hate, will not just leave whilst physical frame dies as the thoughts and intellect and Chitta are nevertheless there. So, we seek situations beneath which we can fulfill our emotional needs and fulfill the bodily goals. So, when we need to meet them, we searching for such an surroundings in order to satisfy our desires, wishes and many others. We as ASTRAL and Causal frame along with thoughts and intellect ego and many others. Which are components of the Astral body, are trying to find OUR PARTENTS. If I need to be musician, I will are seeking musically inclined family. So, the game is like MATCHING GAME can be like eHarmony or matching for medical residency. We have OUR requirements, wishes and choices Karmic end result and money owed and our parents primarily based on their Karma and their goals and their attachments- have their alternatives. When those two suit, the soul enters the brand new fertilized egg or new bodily body. Since further to the pleasure of the desires, we additionally have emotional attachments and debt that we've encountered. So, it is feasible that many deep relationships might be repeated in future lives -even though the bodily frame relationships could change. The siblings is probably satisfactory friends or associates and many others. In next lifestyles. At what exact time this takes place isn't always very clear. Some agree with that the soul can change its mind and so early abortion can show up. Some feel that this takes place when the neural grove is forming, and it closes. The old soul along with its thoughts and its desires and attachments enters new bodily frame to fulfill the needs the goals and repay the debts that turned into created in preceding lives. In the e-book written by way of Dr Brian Weiss, titled Many lives -Many Master, the problem talks approximately something like seventy-two previous lives.

(A foot observe it seems that the soul has a preference of leaving the frame earlier on and so in first few days or weeks and abortion may happen without information of the mother. Secondly the soul does now not necessarily enter the fertilized egg right away. Otherwise, we've got loads of fertilized eggs in lab preserved and the souls could be 'trapped' in them. So, it seems that the preliminary part of one cellular embryo becoming multicell is automatic process and does no longer want the SOUL-Astral-Causal body combination. I do no longer need to get in the dialogue of SOUL or JIVA at this time as in order to confuse our present dialogue)

One can examine this situation to going to a special kind of on line casino but in a unique manner. In common on line casino we cross and play slot machines and wish that we can win large. But as an alternative, in this special on line casino, if we're informed that when you visit casino, each time you touch a slot gadget with intension of triumphing, you may get a chip irrespective of the outcome of the slot device. If you win at the gadget, so one can be extra chips and your aim is to be left with NO CHIPS. Otherwise, you should come to on line casino again. Do you believe you studied it's far ever viable? We will play the slot device and might win some and lose a few, but in this case, we are gaining chip whenever we play the system. So, in our lifestyles touching system is DOING KARMA or ACTION. Winning the slot device game is the attachment that we've while we do Karma or any motion. The casino is the mortal bodily global. So, you can actually never exhaust the chips or Karma, unless there is a way to not gain chip notwithstanding gambling the slot gadget. This is as compared to doing no Karma. But this is nearly not possible. So, one have to come again and back to the on line casino- mortal word. But if one plays with no

DESIRE to win the slot system game, then we will STOP generating new chips – new Karma and eventually we are able to be left and not using a chips or Karma that have any culmination. Remember you advantage chips only whilst you play to win. I.E., you create extra attachments and have effects of your Karma while you ALLOW it to happen. Some humans name it Roasting the Seeds of Karma as Roasted seeds cannot germinate.

One may question as to the proof for this notion method and seeing that we can't communicate (physically) with lifeless people, one should rely upon different indirect ways. The genes and natures and other factors were addressed later can give us oblique proof for such an Action-Reaction results. But we are able to look at lives of many saints a few Indians some non-Indians, one need to have a ZERO balance at the stability sheet of the Karma, then most effective he can stop the rebirth. Zero stability way there's no Karma this is ready to come to fruition. This will occur best while Karmas are completed with no expectation of any desires or expectation and one that had been executed with expectation have already given the fruit. If one looks at lifestyles of Jesus Christ and the resurrection, one wonders as to why did he suffer bodily in this lifestyles. The solution that he became crucified for OUR SINS does not satisfy regular logic. (How can he Know what sins we are going to do in future lives. If the answer is that he's GOD, and God knows EVERYTHING, is not very pleasing. If that is actual, that HE knows the entirety and so he might realize what we are going to do in FUTURE then meaning our lives are PREDETERMINED and we do now not have a choice to do things proper or now not do sins. If we're paying for the sins of Adam and Eve, that defies not unusual feel. Why could I be buying my super-awesome grandparent's sins? My reason behind the story of Adam and Eve in which they sinned and given that whole mankind is descendants of Adam and Eve we are struggling for his or her sins, is lots distinct. The Garden of Eden is the physical body and the tree inside the center of the lawn is experience organs or especially SEX organs. Human beings and can be chimps are the simplest animals who interact in sexual interest as a sense organ satisfaction and now not for need of reproduction. Other animals have intercourse most effective while the female is in warmth. This attachment to sex or sense organ pride is the Universal Sin. In the story when they tasted the fruit, they started masking themselves with leaves. That shows that they were getting excited when they saw each other bare. So, our sin is sense organ attachment and that results in the greater Karma and Desires and that results in rebirth.) When one appears at the lives of many Indian saints, the same form of story repeats. In case of Sai Baba or MEERABAI and many others, whilst one seems at the lives of those saints, we see that they SUFFER in mortal word. If they were notable devotee, then why did they go through?

The answer is in reincarnation. One ought to make his stability sheet zero earlier than she or he has Nirvana or freedom from cycle of demise and beginning. My rationalization is based on Law of Karma -one ought to exhaust all the culmination of past Karmas earlier than he has Freedom from the cycle of life and dying. In case of Jesus Christ or Sai Baba they did now not need their frame to be touched by means of all people for 3 days. So, it appears to me that 3 days are had to neutralize the beyond Karma for theses advanced souls. The Abrahamic religions do no longer have Reincarnation. But one can not be given that the Merciful God could allow us -his youngsters simplest ONE CHANCE to skip or redeem ourselves there's no opportunity to rebirth. We need to try and retry till we are a success.

The query may additionally rise up as to if we get what we DESIRE, then why we see those who are suffering? Did they desire to have the ones suffering? We see those who are blind or handicapped or mentally challenged. I do now not have answer to this question as far as a selected case or someone. But couple of examples from some different resources that

I had encounter will assist to understand. Again, these are not my own examples. One lady became having an eye fixed trouble – may be cataract or glaucoma and she wanted surgical treatment. The lady turned into old, and she or he had lost her most effective son to an twist of fate, and he or she became depressed. She had no close loved ones and felt that having eyesight become now not going to alternate some thing in her existence and she or he refused to have surgery. She felt that there has been nothing left for her to look as she had lost her son. If this intense DESIRE "no longer to see "might persist for prolonged period and specially on the time of loss of life, she may have blindness in her destiny existence. This is natural hypothesis on my element, and I do now not have any evidence. The other example that I examine it someplace that's once more a speculation.

One more tale to provide an explanation for the good judgment at the back of the concept of our dreams coming true in subsequent life. There turned into this mother who had a baby who turned into three-4 years vintage, however the mom had to do the whole thing for the kid. Bathing and feeding and converting diapers and many others. The infant changed into not progressing in its improvement as normal. So, she turned into frustrated. She decided to visit a Swamiji and sked him as to what she must have carried out in remaining life as to get such punishment.

The Swamiji being an Indian and this tale going on in India responded that 'you may had been mom-in-regulation on your closing life and the kid may additionally have been daughter in regulation. And you have to have requested the daughter in regulation to clean garments and convey in tea and cook dinner and do the laundry and so forth. So now it's time to repay."

The mother become smart and asked, 'That sounds logical, however then why is my daughter in law who did the whole lot for me in ultimate lifestyles is struggling now and cannot have a normal lifestyles?'

The Swamiji responded, 'Yes, it's miles real that she the daughter in law did the whole lot for you, but whenever she did it, she was questioning that I desire I could get this again and feature my mother-in-law do this stuff for me. So, she is now getting it again.'

The moral of the story is simple. When we do something, we should do it without a expectation or attachment for the coolest deed that we did, in any other case it's going to create the bondage and then rebirth is assured.

WHY DO WE COME BACK – WHY REBIRTH?

I even have informed the answer to this question above. But one may nevertheless have questions as to why we come back in bodily form when we KNOW that with a purpose to INCREASE the KARMAS and that will cause greater Impressions and that in flip will result in More DESIRES which makes

NIRVAN OR MOKSHA VERY DIFFICULT OR IMPOSSIBLE. Rebirth can be compared to having more credit cards and taking more loans to pay off it and as we boom the debt, we don't have any chance of DEBT FREE fame. So, in spite of these dangers, why do we come back? The answer lies in what I said as WHAT CONSTITUTES KARMA. Remember the PHYSICAL ACTION results in Karma and intellectual ACTION ALONE IS NOT LIKRLY TO BE Karma except it is intense and repeated. If after the dying of physical frame, we have no Physical frame how we are able to do Good Karmas of supporting a person as maximum of our assistance is for bodily elements like pain, infection, most cancers, hunger, pain, and so forth. So, if we need to do extra of precise Karmas, we have to have Physical frame and then simplest we will INCREASE correct Karmas. Someone may additionally say that we additionally have mental suffering and even if we do not have physical body, we do have Astral frame -SUKSHMA SHARIR, which has Mind, Intellect and Ego. So, we may want to help a person via calming the Mind.

But maximum of the time intellectual affliction is due to or associated with bodily problems. We experience awful due to loss of buddy or relatives or activity or may be because of loss of money or food or huge house – car and so on. All these items are in a manner related to PHYSICAL UNIVERSE and although we have sadness which is in our Mind, the remedy or the assist isn't just for the thoughts unless we contend with the issues that occurred in Physical Universe. As I said in beyond, we create DEBT while we've RELATIONSHIPS. We assist someone, we love someone, we hate a person, and we take money -meals -safe haven -help from someone or offer the equal to others. This creates debt. This must be repaid. So try this we need physical body.

CAN ONE REGRESS FROM BEING HUMAN BEINGS TO ANIMAL

One of the frequent questions that we get while we speak about reincarnation is that 'Do we usually come lower back as Human beings, or can we come back as other species? If we do come again as Human beings, then had been we ever born as animals?' The solution to this query lies in a concept. This is my idea or concept, and someone will have different concept technique. Do animals have Law of Karma implemented to them? As I cited before, the animal nation is referred to as BHOGA YONI. I experience that Human beings have developed cognizance. The animals act on instincts and do now not plan an awful lot for destiny as such. We store meals and water. We hoard and gather and keep cash. We build shelters and make them extra comfortable by having warmth or Air conditioning. But the animals do not do such a thing. They do no longer plan, and they act on intuition. Most of the animals interact in sexual act simplest when the girl is in warmness. So, they act on intuition. So, the Law of Karma does now not practice at all at worst and applies at very minimal stage at nice. I say this as no longer all of the animals have SIMILER existence. Some of the dogs' sleep of their master's mattress and different are wandering in street looking for food and some are taken to pound. They all have sicknesses and illness and we do see them suffering bodily and mentally. So, there should be some Law that controls their life. But we do not know. So., I think there should be some connection. I do consider that there's Law of Karma that does apply to animals but no longer on the equal quantity as Human beings. This does not suggest there are two one-of-a-kind Laws - one for Himan beings and different for animal state. The Intent of any action is critical in figuring out the outcomes of the motion. Since we do not realize the Intent of movement via animal, we won't recognise the reaction. For example, if a canine bites a infant -did it do a bad karma? The answer lies in why did the dog chunk. If the child pulled the tail and the canine acted as a defense, then it'll not have equal consequences as if the dog had attacked the kid who become simply gambling alone. The tiger attacking a expensive for food is exceptional than we kill someone out of anger. Each animal has a few good and a few awful VASANAS or desires. Dog is loyal and shielding for his master. The pig is grimy, and fox is foxy etc. There are 8400000 extraordinary lifestyles paperwork described in Hindu faith. So, we are supposed to EXHUAST our Vasanas going through the life in animal kingdom and then whilst we attain the Human lifestyles, we are alleged to do better than having those Vasanas or desires. But if one continues to make major mistakes like serial killers or rapist, then there's no way that they are able to repay the debt in one or many lives as he or she will preserve to build up more karmic results. So, she or he have to REGRESS in animal kingdom in which maximum of the actions are based totally on instinct and so the effect of those Karma is restricted. This may be as compared to one having a debt of cash which needs to be repaid. But if the debt is such that one can't repay it, then he need to declare Bankruptcy. When one has declared the bankruptcy then the creditors prevent. Same manner when one regresses to animal nation the regulation of karma will become limited or weak or stops and you'll be able to pay off the debt. In majority of cases once a soul reaches human form, they'll continue to be born as human beings. THIS IS ONLY MY THOUGHT.

Many a instances human beings quate from Bhagwat Geeta a verse which states in bankruptcy 2 verse forty2-47

You have only the proper to work, but in no way to its culmination.

Let no longer the fruits of action be your cause, nor let your attachment be to inactiveness.

This verse is well-known and as in line with my understanding is misinterpreted most of the time. As stated above the which means is that once You do Karma, you do now not have right to the Fruits of Your Action or Karma, but you've got right to the motion best. So, do not do Action -Karma with expectation of the Fruits, however then it also states that Do no longer have INACTION.

One would possibly finish that one have to stop having any expectation for his movement or any fruits from the Karma which you do. But this isn't the which means. Think approximately a situation. You call a person to color the house and he does paint the residence. So, do now not you watched that he's going to EXPECT the money for his paintings -the so called the end result of his motion? So, in each state of affairs in existence when we do a little movement, we count on the consequences from it and honestly there may be nothing wrong with it, however in addition to that, we count on REWARD for our so-referred to as GOOD action or Karma. Say I observe difficult for the exam, I will count on that I will get suitable marks. So why would this verse country that DO NOT count on culmination of movement. I feel that what it's far stating is that there may be going to be a few fruit to your Action or Karma climate you need it. Expect it or ACCEPT it. So, there is no escape from the culmination. So, you do not have RIGHT to get it or reject the fruit. It is telling us that one ought to no longer do an motion with reason to get the fruits that You need. If we do now not do any movement with DESIRE for the culmination, then that Karma or Action is like roasted seed if you want to no longer sprout a tree. So, while we do Karma, we sou the seed and there could be plant popping out of it and there can be fruits. But if the seed is roasted then there will no longer be any plant and so there could be no fruit. THIS IS THE ONLY WAY FOR DOING KARMA AND HAVE NO FRUITS. So, the detachment can be the most effective solution. The other preference, one might imagine to no longer get fruit or have outcomes of 1's motion is to NOT DO ANY ACTION. So, in 2nd line HE tells us that HE isn't always advising INACTION as option to keep away from getting culmination. One can not stop all the sports of each day life of livings and so when ordinary guy does any motion, he has expectation to get top fruits of his accurate action after which he gets attachments after which when he gets the rewards, he is glad after which that Impression of happiness or SUKH results in preference to do more movement with expectation to correct fruits. This intensifies the results of Karma and desires and then there is no freedom from the cycles of beginning and loss of life. So, the solution is to Do Karma and provide the culmination to the God. If we retain to do Karma and anticipate rewards, there may be no freedom.

To apprehend the Freedom from cycle of birth and dying, one should know the concept of three bodies. Swami Yoganand at one time gave an example to recognize the shape of the body and the manner to get freedom. (This is that this his instance). If one fills a pitcher bottle with ocean water and seals it and places in another bottle and seals that second bottle and then positioned these two bottles in some other bottle and seals it, this is just like the three bodies and the SELF. If one drops those bottles in ocean, the water inside the innermost bottle is similar to one in ocean, but it can not blend with it and has FEELING of being cut loose the sea water. So, even though the self is equal as general attention, it IDENTIFIES with the Physical frame additionally called STHULA SHARIR. The outer maximum bottle is like Physical frame and this is damaged on the time of demise. But the SELF isn't unfastened as it's miles enclosed in different our bodies specifically ASTRAL-additionally called SUKSHMA OR SUBTLE BODY and CAUSAL also known as KARAN SHARIR bodies. (Or it feels it is limited with the aid of the three bodies -that is JIV- This is a sincere way to recognize. Consciousness is by no means LIMITED and pervades the entirety) One need to ruin all 3 bottles, then best the water can be combined with whole ocean water -and not using a separate lifestyles. Under regular occasions the SELF (while it identifies with those bodies it's far known as JIV or JIVATMA) along with the 2 our bodies continues from one lifestyles to different. Only way to set SELF loose is to break all 3 bottles. As long as one keeps to do Karma with expectation of end result of action and getting connected to the fruits of motion theses bottles – our bodies cannot be damaged.

So, one must do KARMA – ACTION and not using a attachments to the end result of Action. Just to repeat the FRUITS will usually be there. But if we keep away from the attachments to them, we are able to not have their impressions which in turn create Desires.

A brief rationalization of 3 bodies can be needed for humans who have not heard of this idea. The names are self-explanatory. The Physical frame is thought to each person and does now not need any similarly clarification. All have Mind and questioning and intellect and emotions and feeling etc. This is the Subtle Body. Again, this is simple to recognize. The CAUSE for the existence of these thoughts and feelings and feeling is CAUSAL BODY as that is the reason for the alternative our bodies.

I will deliver one greater example to recognize. Let us take an instance of a reflect. The replicate is an regular glass which has been coated on one aspect, so that it reflects the mild and causes picture. When we positioned this sort of covered glass-the replicate in a body we've got the mirrors which can be bought in market. The body of this reflect can be in comparison to the Physical frame, the Glass itself to the Astral body and the coating cloth to the Causal frame. So, the coating material CAUSES the regular glass to be a replicate. The Glass displays and so that is Astral frame and the frame which can be CHANGED is just like the Physical frame -which may be modified with every birth-death cycle. When we see the mirrored image of SUN, the reflection seems like real Sun, however it isn't and that can be in comparison to the SELF which in a manner is the reflection of the general attention. This is PARAMATMA and the photograph is Jivatma. The SELF sheds mild in order that the three bodies can function. But it itself does now not do anything. Without the meditated mild from the reflect, one can't see anything. But the Sunlight that's contemplated with the aid of the mirror from the photo of Sun isn't always REAL sun. This is straightforward instance. As lengthy as there may be Sun and we've replicate, we are able to have the photo of the real Sun, and this can have the reflected light. As is with all the examples they have got a few pitfalls, but that is as near as it may get. Without the Real Sun, there may be no contemplated Sun and there is no light, and one cannot see.

The example of the SUN and the pots packed with water is old and popular. So, there are numerous pots packed with water and all will have reflection of the SUN. The real Sun isn't there however with out pot and the water, the SUN can't be visible. This is as compared to the extraordinary bodily bodies and the same Sun or the recognition or so-known as Purusha. Without the water, Sun can't be visible. The water is like ASTRAL or subtle body and without the diffused frame, the Sun cannot shine (But the SUN IS STILL THERE). The Sun isn't worried in any manner but without the Sun, there may be no Light -Life. So, to have a LIVE PERSON we want the Sun or the Purusha and desires ASTRAL BODY.

I heard every other instance for cutting-edge existence. We are like a computer; The hardware is like physical frame. One could even say that the CPU is like brain. The software is like ASTRAL or Subtle frame. So, without the software program the pc is useless – it will no longer characteristic. The hardware can be ideal but no software program to make it do matters. Now consider the software disc with memory The disk, that's part of Hardware, has weight. But the software program that you upload does now not INCREASE the burden of the difficult force. The same issue is real about the SUBTLE BODY or CAUSAL BODY. It has all of the reminiscence and the impressions- of the Karma, and mind, mind. But all this stuff are NOT PHYSICAL and so it does not have any weight. But similar to without software the pc will not paintings, the physical body will now not paintings without the Astral Body. Now think about a state of affairs, where the laptop has been plugged in, has hardware, and has software. It will paintings fine. But if there may be no strength the pc will no longer work. Despite having software program and hardware the computer will now not feature if there is no strength or a electricity source like battery. But the electricity itself does now not do the work of laptop. When it is connected to a fan, the fan works, if it's far connected to AC, the AC works, if it is connected to heater, the heater works. The electricity can be considered as the ALL-PERVADING CONSCIOUSNESS. The strength can run many computer systems - identical with the attention. But once more, without software program the energy will not do any work of the computer. So, it is the aggregate of strength and the software program then most effective the computer works. Similarly, the recognition and Astral body are needed in bodily body to have normal physical body characteristic.

(I referred to this as there was experiments to discover the burden of SOUL or anything that leaves the bodily frame. Many years ago, someone did an test wherein he weighed someone while they were on demise bed and proper once they dies. The weight distinction is twenty-one grams, So the conclusion became that soul weighs. Then these experiments had been finished with sheep and the weight was distinct and next experiments could not substantiate the same outcomes. I simply noted it as I stated that the Astral and Causal body do now not have any weight.)

The focus in Vedic faith, is infinite. There are three things, by way of which gadgets are restricted specifically, DESH -KAL VASTU. DESH method predicament of area. KAL manner drawback of time and VASTU method quandary of identity. If I take an example of anything round us like sofa that I am sitting on, it has limits of all three. The sofa is in my family room and no longer in dwelling room or anywhere else. So, it is constrained being simply here and it cannot be everywhere else at a given time. The consciousness has no such trouble as it's miles ALL OVER AT THE SAME TIME. There isn't any PLACE in which the consciousness isn't there. So, the sofa has dilemma of DESH or limitation of the distance. The sofa is converting all of the time. It was new the day gone by and now it's miles older, and it'll be very old tomorrow and will no longer be there in future. So, it has issue of TME -KAL. But the recognition has no such dilemma. The Consciousness does now not CHANGE EVER. And lastly the couch is best SOFA and not TV, desk, or chair. So, it has hindrance of VASTU or an item. It is best one aspect and not something else. But the attention isn't an Object and does now not have such trouble.

(But as I stated earlier than the recognition wishes unit of thoughts- mind-ego-Chitta to have any expression or experience. The recognition can not do anything as it does now not have any choice and it cannot be perceived as anything that may be perceived isn't Consciousness. The focus is there even in dead body however there is no unit of thoughts-intellect-ego and so the bodily frame even though bodily present, can not understand as there may be no Astral or

SUKSHMA frame. So useless physical body is DEAD BODY!

SOME OF THE EXAMPLES OF LAW OF KARMA AND REINCARNATION

1 Everyone who's acquainted with the Mahabharat, knows that there were kings Pandu and Dhritarashtra. The Dhritarashtra became blind, and he had a hundred sons who were called Kauravas, and Pandu had five or 6 sons and they have been known as Pandawas. Metaphorically the Dhritarashtra – the Blind king represents BLIND thoughts as mind acts blindly and does now not continually think of effects. The Pandu represents Intellect that is CLEAR or WHITE and so the king Pandu was white in shade. But the story as to how the Dhritarashtra became blind is related to Reincarnation and Law of karma. In past life or one of the lives, the King become a hunter, and he went to woodland, and he desired to get a few birds. He noticed a tree where there were masses of birds with nest. He began a fireplace beneath the tree

and as the tree caught the fire the tiny birds misplaced eyesight, and some died. This act caused the impact that he became born blind, and he had one hundred sons and he had to suffer the loss of all a hundred sons, similar to the bird who misplaced the young one inside the nest while he had set fireplace to the tree. So, the results of Karma got here to fruition in special life, and one cannot keep away from it.

2 Everyone know Lord Ram and his father. The father turned into a king named Dasharath. One day he had long past for looking. He changed into sitting hiding on a department of a tree. There turned into lake and he predicted that a wild animal will come for consuming water, and he's going to do the searching. As it took place, there was a younger boy named Shravan, who became taking his blind dad and mom to pilgrimage. He had stopped close by, and he got here to the lake to fetch the water for the thirsty parents. He had a pot and as he positioned the pot inside the water it produced the

sound. King Dasharath couldn't see however the sound he heard, convinced him that there was an animal drinking the water and he shot an arrow in the path of the sound. The end result become a human being shouting in pain. Immediately he got here down from the tree, ran to the lake, and realized the error whilst he discovered out that it turned into certainly a boy. The boy advised him approximately the parents after which died. He went to the parents. They could not see him however then he defined the state of affairs and requested for forgiveness. The dad and mom had been mad and told him that they're going to die with sorrow of losing their only son and he's going to additionally die of sorrow of dropping his son. As it took place King Dashrath did not have any children at that point. But in future he had the youngsters and when eldest son -Lord Ram needed to go away for VANAWAS for 14 years and he died of sorrow of separation. So, again the Karma had the outcomes and he had to pay back or saw the impact within the identical lifestyles.

3, In Satyanarayan Katha we have 5 specific chapters, and the principle characters are reborn in next lifestyles as extraordinary humans. The antique Brahmin who turned into poor and turned into blessed by means of the Lord became reborn as Sudama -Lord Krishna's friend after which changed into provided lots of money. The Wood cutter took delivery as Guha who occur to hold Lord Ram across the river in his boat. So, every body were given rewards for their motion. Unconditional love for God brought them closure to God.

Now a few questions and possible answers.

1 Is there difference between movement executed on my own and an motion completed on my component?

The brief solution is YES. So, if a king or president orders an assault through the infantrymen, is the king or the president answerable for the moves of the squaddies. The solution is YES. There is idea that when one is appearing his obligation and has do so sure things which are considered bad or terrible karma, aren't considered as awful as the individual is doing it as a part of Duty. This is going each methods -precise and terrible. So, I devour meat and I do not hunt or kill animals for food, but I pass and buy the meat from supermarket. I am responsible for the killing of animals? The solution is YES. Direct killing is worse however eating meat that changed into from an animal killed via a person else is also horrific Karma. As I stated any degree of this method is Bad Karma-selling -killing -cooking and consuming meat will have some horrific Karma.

Now on the alternative aspect of the equation. The Good Karma or Punya -the degree of it varies as to who is doing it. If I do the POOJA and worship, that is the pleasant way.(Best if I don't ASK for something) If I do it via a clergyman that reduces the PUNYA, and if I do it for advantage of a person else like my son or daughter, it is not as desirable as me doing it for myself and if I ask a priest to do it for a person else, it isn't always as suitable as or has the consequences as it might have if the man or woman does it himself for himself. But once more, although one gets the credit – the Punya, it's going to sow the seeds and it will have reaction and so it will fructify.

So, the movement may have effect and the reaction to the movement is proportional to the motion and so if I kill myself there might be greater impact and if I worship then the reaction may be extra.

2 If each Karma has response and impact and that MUST come to fruition from time to time in future, on this lifestyles or destiny lives then how can one get out of this cycle of beginning and demise.

This is a question that involves mind each time a person is told that Every Karma could have reaction and response. When we have the reaction to our previous action/Karma, we do extra Action or Karma after which that adds to the response or reaction. So, that is like taking a loan from a loan shark. The hobby is so excessive that all the money is wasted in repaying the interest and the original debt is not paid at all and the interest maintains to build up. So how can we forestall this worsening debt of Karma?

There is a way. But it is very difficult and may sound impossible. We have REACTION to our ACTION or Karma as we do motion with EXPECTATION or attachment to the response. When we pray, we anticipate the God to reward us with what we prayed for or for a few benefit like advertising in activity or commercial enterprise achievement or something for our circle of relatives etc. This expectation ends in attachment -if we get what we requested for then we get attached to it. If we do not get what we asked for then we have bad attachment -or called aversion to what we were given. So, this provides to more Karma. So, if we pray just because we are dedicated to God or do our process as if it's miles our obligation and do now not anticipate 'matters,' then we can prevent the Reaction and that manner the Karma will not have culmination to our Karma and our debt can be repaid.

three Who keeps the records of Karma and their impressions after which reaction.

There are two separate issues or questions. When I do a Karma and that causes an affect, that's in bodily Brain. We recognize that after we devour a cake and like it, our brain has the affect and that creates the desire to devour it again. This is well known. But the equal influence is also saved in astral brain / body in summary form. (Or can be Causal Body) With the dying of physical body and the physical brain, the precise influence for the flavor of cake is long gone. But the summary form of that cake- sweetness, the texture, or the odor- some thing you appreciated – is there in astral mind. The Astral frame is in no way destroyed except one has Nirvana or MUKTI because the astral frame is carried from one existence to other. Astral – causal frame has mind and intellect and Chitta with it and so this is wherein the statistics are stored. This is a Law. When we throw a ball in air, it comes down to floor due to the force of gravity. We never ask a query as to how a ball is aware of about the Laws of gravity. The equal way the Law of Karma is there, and we're all sure via it -weather we find it irresistible or no longer, we be given it or now not.

4 Can equal Karma have distinct effect or fruit?

This is a question that is often raised as we see in our existence two extraordinary humans doing same non secular ritual and get extraordinary results. We additionally see humans doing non-non secular interest, which are comparable, but have distinctive outcome. There are as a minimum special answers.

A)As became cited in the sooner a part of this e-book, there are two awesome components to doing a Karma. One is intellectual and second is physical. We interact in natural bodily activity or Karma and natural mental concept method or Karma, and we sincerely have Karma where each intellectual and bodily Karma are blended. We can increase our hand or listen to a new type of music - these are almost natural Physical movement with now not much mental concept. Then we've only intellectual procedure or karma-as an instance- we suppose all of the time approximately different things – triumphing a lottery or about a person-our boss or baby-kisser or neighbor or our partner. Again, most of the time that is best intellectual technique or Karma. When the mental concept is combined with bodily motion, the impact is maximum suggested. The intellectual notion may be equal or extraordinary. So, while the notion in the back of the motion is exclusive the outcomes might be distinct. Let us take an instance of a easy prayer to the God. One character prays God to get some thing for himself – cash -electricity-success in commercial enterprise- the impact or the fruit of this prayer will be exceptional than whilst someone does the prayer with an intension or choice to damage someone-that a person can have a terrible success -now not get a process or fail in an exam or failure in love and so on. One is accomplished with intension of getting right success for oneself or his own family – pal, the other is executed with a desire to have unwell destiny for someone that he does no longer like or hate. And finally one does a prayer to the God sincerely because of the affection for the God and haven't any expectation. The outcomes of the equal motion or end result of the equal prayer are extraordinary. This is one explanation of having one-of-a-kind culmination to the equal action or Karma. WHAT IS THE INTENSION BEHIND THE PRAYER OR ACTION?

B)I have also noted the unseen pressure from PREVIOUS Karmas which are going to come to fruition in this existence -called PRARABDHA Karma. This is unknown and it'll regulate the final results of our gift lifestyles Karma - KRIYAMAN Karma. So, I may be supporting someone and expect that he's going to admire it but that does not happen – may be because of his and your previous dating in this life or final lifestyles. We know how suspicious we're while someone who has attempted to damage us in beyond, all of sudden wants to assist and we aren't very receptive. Here we KNOW what took place in beyond and so our response is expected and does no longer come as a marvel to the other man or woman. But think about the identical type of conduct that can have happened in past life and we aren't aware of it. So, then we do no longer recognise the preceding action and so we're amazed by using the reaction that is combination of present Karma and end result of ultimate existence Karma. So, this undercurrent of preceding Karmas alters the direction or the rate of present existence Karma.

five. There is every other component that I would like to point out. The Karma will always supply its fruit and that could never be avoided. Sometimes the end result look unique in different humans, and it is able to now not be apparent to us because the response to the motion or the fruit because the result of identical action. One of the examples can be lacking a meal as an effect of some Karma. If the person is Sattvic – full of true deeds in gift lifestyles, he's going to still have the same impact as missing the meal, but it may be voluntary, and he may be fasting as non secular ritual as the reason for lacking the meal or perhaps he become assisting pals and neglected the meals as he became busy whilst he become supporting in their health troubles or monetary problems and so on. Contrary to that if he's of terrible inclinations – TAMASIC inclinations, then he may additionally omit a meal because of combat with circle of relatives and getting mad etc. And the Rajasic dispositions man or woman may be too busy with workplace or meetings or business. So, the consequences will be there, but it can be different if the host has distinct nature. The identical element can be discovered if the fruit is fantastic like getting cash. How a person receives the cash will relies upon upon what GUNAS or inclinations the person has. If he's Sattvic, Positive traits then he may additionally win lottery or get money from a few individual as appreciation for the things he's doing for community. If he is of Tamasic traits, then he can also steal or get it as ransom or bribe. If he has Rajasic satisfactory, then he will get the identical cash with the aid of doing a little enterprise offers.

One component to consider approximately the fruits of movement or Karma is that when the fruit has appeared we have no desire however to simply accept it and then that Karma is gone. WE CANNOT POST PONE OR PREPONE the results. If we donated money to a charity and that they posted a listing of the doners or thanked us in public and many others., the Fruits of our Good deeds or Karma has been accomplished with. We can not assume that our suitable deed or Karma will be giving us Good Luck in destiny. So, anonymous donation is first-rate as that Good Karma can ripe or fructify in future rather than having call brought to the listing of doners on the wall of church or temple.

6 Can you do any new Karma while we do no longer have bodily frame?

This question is like the one we discussed. Why can we come back? We lose the bodily body while at the time of loss of life, we're alleged to have Astral body or SUKHSMA SHARIR and the Causal or KARAN SHARIR. We are in Astral World and there are very few or no situations while we are able to do top Karma or Bad Karma. Normally we've issues with physical body and despite the fact that thoughts isn't always a part of bodily body, it can't do much if there is no physical frame. I may additionally want to enjoy ice cream. My mind has a memory of precise flavor of ice cream and so I need to eat it. But if I do not have physical hands and bodily tongue, I can not get ice cream from Freeze and eat it to experience it. So, NO PHYSICAL BODY – NO ENJOYEMENT OF ICE CREAM. Suppose I am mad at a person, and I need to harm him, which I can't do – I can't hit him with out bodily frame. Most of the time the help we do is for bodily body and maximum of the time we do terrible things also are for bodily body e.G., ravenous or disease or cancer or any pain etc. So, we cannot do plenty as PUNYA or PAP- proper or terrible Karma whilst we do now not have physical frame. So, we have confined alternatives whilst we do no longer have bodily frame to do any KARMA. So, we have to come back to mortal international of Physical our bodies to do new Good or Bad Karma.

7.Can the KARMAS of mother and father have an effect on the lifestyles of their kids?

When we take a look at this question superficially, query in everyday lifestyles – with out thinking about the Law of Karma-is not a query at all. The lifestyles of parents will have an effect on the life of youngsters. If the dad and mom are knowledgeable children are much more likely to be knowledgeable. If dad and mom smoke or have alcoholism, then the children are much more likely to smoke or drink alcohol. But the query is not if the ACTIONS of dad and mom affect the lifestyles of their children, however can the closing life Karma of mother and father have an effect on the lifestyles of kids? The solution is YES. But now not inside the same way as one may think. As I noted above, one SELECTS THE PARENTS and not the other way spherical. We as soul or Jivatma with Astral Body and Causal frame with out physical frame, (the circumstance that is present after death) must come to mortal international, to meet our desires and repay the debt. The relationships that parents have with their youngsters, or siblings have with each other's, or spouses have with every different or buddies etc. Will be a pressure to carry us again collectively. But the handiest element that we will SELECT whilst we pick to be borne are parents. Rest of the relationships are not some thing that we can pick out. But one of the matters that one may additionally misunderstand from this description is that WE GET SAME PARTENTS IN ALL LIVES. That isn't what I am announcing. Our current parents can also had been our grandparents or friends or our buddies or another relationships in beyond life, which evolved sure 'provide and take' or debt and positive situations that would assist us fulfill our unfulfilled desires. But as a great deal as WE have goals and desires, the dad and mom have also desires and want and while those two fits we are borne to that set of mother and father. So, the end result of Karma of parents have some thing in common with that of children and in order that manner the Karma and their culmination which might be coming to fruition in present life must have some thing in commonplace with that of children and in order that they do have an effect on every other's life.

8. What approximately the FERTISED EGGS which might be saved in labs, do they've soul?

This query has stricken me for long time. Since for any movement to be considered as Karma, it should be completed by means of a Living being. So, while the eggs are fertilized in check tube and then saved for destiny implantation in uterus, is there soul this is going to see consequences of Karma from remaining lives? I do not have a clear-cut answer and couldn't locate from any found out or developed souls. But I have some mind and I will tell them. When the egg is fertilized, a seed for production of grownup animal if it's far human embryo then it's far individual, is shaped. It clearly has potential for growing into human beings. But does it have a soul? Based on what I even have stated above, the soul in Astral global seeks the proper womb/ occasions to meet unfulfilled dreams, it need to know the situations that he or she will be able to have. So, if the embryo isn't implanted in any womb, it cannot recognise the instances. So, it could now not be in function to choose. So despite the fact that the egg is fertilized, except it is implanted, the soul will no longer input. If the soul enters at time of fertilization, then whilst those embryos are stored in lab, some of these souls will be 'trapped 'for years, as many unclaimed or un implanted embryos are stored in lab. When the fertilization occurs in vivo and no longer vitro, the soul does recognize the dad and mom and occasions and can input faster and now not wait. But again, it is able to alternate the mind and so it may leave or no longer enter in any respect and so many abortions arise tremendously early, and all that mom knows is her length became not on time for couple of weeks.

(I need to do some rationalization of the word SOUL. This is an English word and there is a bent for most people to apply it interchangeably with words from Vedic faith like ATMAN, SELF or JIVA or JIVATMA. But there may be no Perfect phrase which could describe word soul as defined in English. The focus pervades everything and whilst it is 'trapped' in a frame or restrained to frame and due to lack of know-how thinks that it isn't free and not all pervading, it limits itself to the frame and so the PARAMATMA turns into Jivatma or Jiva or the soul. The 'Unit 'of SUKSHMA SHARIR – Astral or Subtle Body, which has mind – mind -ego and the KARANA SHARIR – Causal Body -travels from one body to other. Since the cognizance is there anywhere and whilst there may be connection among the consciousness and the Astral and causal frame then the LIFE takes place. So, the fertilized egg in Lab or in human frame, could have cognizance as THERE IS NO PLACE WHERE CONSCIOUSNESS IS NOT THERE. It does now not have the difficulty of DESH-KAL-VASTU- Desha means quandary by way of vicinity -I am right here and now not there or this laptop is right here and no longer in my workplace, Kal approach drawback via time- which means some thing is there nowadays and no longer the next day the chair that I am sitting was not there a 12 months in the past and will now not be there in 5 years and ultimately Vaastu difficulty - because of this chair is a chair and not a laptop and laptop is pc and no longer pizza . Everything in this world has those three obstacles and CONSCIOUSNESS does not have them. So, the Consciousness is there in the whole lot and anywhere, however the soul isn't there inside the sense as we use the phrase soul.)

9.Is there Soul in person who is in a vegetative nation?

We have frequently seen patients who pass in coma and do not reply to verbal stimuli or any physical activity on command. So is there a soul and is there any Karma coming to fruition. Is that physical body repaying for some previous Karma? If there may be no Soul, then there might be no 'suffering' and there's no repaying of the previous debt. This is remarkably thrilling question. I have my 'opinion and it's far simply my opinion. What is SELF or CONSCIOUSNESS or the SOUL? Soul is not doing something, but without it nothing happens. So, the mind, mind, or Chitta should do not anything with out the SOUL however the Soul itself does no longer do anything. It is like light. If there was no light, we couldn't do some thing as we couldn't see and do any interest. That does not imply light makes us do whatever. Some people do good matters and a few horrific, however the mild does now not make them do properly or horrible matters. The matters are there around us and

161

we will see them and then act for that reason. But if we did no longer have the eyesight or eyes, no matter light we could not see. The equal with wondering. We have to have mind and SOUL to assume. Now in man or woman with vegetative status, there may be problem with both physical body – like mind harm or can be the mind-mind -Chitta unit is defective, however the soul / attention continues to be there. But without the Instrument of action and notion we can't act. Let me give some other instance. Look on the Christmas mild bulbs chain that we use to enhance at the time of Christmas. The power is wanted for the bulbs to function. But say one of the bulbs is terrible or broken, the complete chain won't work. The relaxation of the bulbs will work independently if checked but due to damaged bulb the complete chain does not work. The electricity continues to be there, and the final bulbs are working, but now not as a unit in a series. So, the strength is like soul or awareness and bulb is like thoughts. Intellect etc. In vegetative man or woman the SOUL IS THERE however the bodily unit is defective and so the unit of thoughts or mind or Chitta can't explicit.

One greater example that I can give may help to understand. The Physical body BORROWS the cognizance, and the feel organs borrow it from the mind. The instance that is given in Vedanta lectures is that of boiling a potato in a water in a pot on a fire. The heat in potato is borrowed from the heated water and the heat in heated water is borrowed from the pot and the pot borrows it from the hearth. So, the fireplace is the SOURCE of the warmth and for relaxation of them it is borrowed belongings. So, we need fire to have potato cooked. But the fire couldn't do some thing if there was no pot, water, or potato. No heat transfer ought to show up.

(There are couple of approaches we can reflect onconsideration on the awareness or the JIVA. The Consciousness is pervading the whole thing but does no longer do ANYTHING by using itself in any everyday life or activities in global. So, it's miles like sunlight which does now not do any interest as such, but it facilitates us to see and then we do the activity. If there has been no Light, we can't see. But if we aren't there then the sunlight will no longer do anything. So, the focus may be there everywhere however without the physical body with its sense organs for notion– subtle frame with its thoughts and mind and causal frame, it cannot do some thing. The Jiva is the consciousness, or its reflection CONFINED to those three bodies or mistakenly identified with these three bodies. So, the attention does not become JIVA till it has three bodies. This might also assist on answers to above questions.)

The soul is focus constrained to a unit of causal- astral and at times physical frame due to lack of knowledge. So despite the fact that recognition is not Limited via DESH -KAL- VASTU -place- time – identification respectively- because of lack of knowledge it gets restrained to a Physical Body. So, then it does 'go through' with suffering of the physical or mental suffering whilst in vegetative popularity.

10. Can ANYONE change the DESTINY like saints or any evolved souls?

I have stated that NO ONE can trade future which is drawing close. No one escapes the results of Law of Karma. I also said that there are 3 types of outcomes or consequences that pop out of movement or karma. Some that may be changed effortlessly and some that can be modified simplest with huge efforts and a few that CANNOT be modified regardless of HEROIC efforts. I additionally said that sure matters which can be going to come back to fruition in very brief time can't be modified as there isn't sufficient time. (The example that I gave was that of examination the following day when the scholar has not studied till today) so, this is real for everyday character who has restrained assets. What about the excellent souls– saints or sages -can they change it? And if they are able to, how can they do that? Is there exception to the first rate Law that I were declaring? We have heard the tales of Jesus who did miracles and the same with many different saints. So how can they negate the effects of Law of Karma and future? The answer is YES- The incredible souls can alternate it. If you examine the Patanjali Sutra Yoga, (to be had on Amazon books beneath my call) the advanced souls do acquire some powers and that they may be used. So, do they nullify the consequences of the Karma? The solution is that they can CHANGE it but no longer AVOID it completely. This is wherein the Law of Reincarnation are available in play. As I said there may be Stored up Karma -SANCHIT Karma and we are borne with some of them to come back to fruition in gift existence referred to as PRARABDHA. So, every existence -and there are heaps of them, and every is with its own PRARABDHA. (I can evaluate this to changing Flu strain each 12 months -it's far nonetheless Flu virus, however it modifications each yr so a few results are distinctive) So those saints and sages can change/shift/delay a number of those outcomes of Karma from one lifestyles to other. So, the effects are there, however INSTEAD OF PRESENT LIFE, they're changed to return to fruition in NEXT LIFE. If someone is going to die in subsequent 3 months or 3 days, theses Sages can BORROW some life from subsequent lifestyles with its attached Karmic effects. This is brief and the person will must face the effects that had been to come back to fruition in this existence and postponed to subsequent lifestyles. So, we do now not AVOID it but just POSTPONE it. We can BORROW the money from bank or mortgage shark, but we can must REPAY it every so often.

eleven. Do Prayers paintings to CHANGE the PRARBDHA?

This query always pops in my mind on every occasion we are doing prayer, ASKING God for some thing for me or my own family. I do not understand when we offer $1 donation for prevailing 1,000,000-dollar lottery. But I do not suppose the prayers will be in comparison to this Give and Take sort of attitude of the prayer. I do believe that the prayers do work, With God's grace and Desire or desire, they do work. The trouble is how do you prove this? We in no way recognise the final results. So, we can not prove or disprove if prayers work. Say we pray to get accurate grade or getting a task for our child etc. How would we understand if the fulfillment become due to the prayers or the result that we see, turned into going to happen because of PRARABDH? One must determine if she or he should pray or no longer, however one component for sure the prayers give internal power, regardless of what the result is. So, if we do prayers with full faith and announcing and believing that it's miles God's desire and benefits, they are effective. Even even though The Karma will provide consequences-no matter what, in an extraordinary circumstances God can intrude like the sages can exchange on uncommon activities.

There had been quantity of studies performed that show that that the prayers do no longer work. I am going to mention some of them and then try and supply my clarification on the consequences. One look at which is probably the oldest, is from 1800. The British Royal Family receives maximum prayers and so Francis Galton did the observe to see if the British Royalty had longer lifestyles span or more healthy existence. Certainly, many people move on saying 'Long Live King' and different such prayers. The query changed into -if so, many people are praying for the King or the Queen, do they live longer than average lifestyles span of British topics for whom no such prayers are performed with the aid of loads. The end turned into that there has been no distinction in the existence expectancy and the diseases had been common in British Royalty. This changed into now not a double-blind prospective look at.

In 2006 Tempelton Foundation did a study of patients undergoing coronary artery skip surgical procedure. This was double blind and changed into multicenter – 6 hospitals have been worried, the wide variety of patients were 1800.Christian prayed for" a hit surgery, brief restoration, and no complications". The devotee or the individuals who prayed have been given the names- last call and first name of the patient for which they have been praying. There had been 3 groups. The first institution become instructed that human beings may also or won't be praying for them even though prayers had been executed for all the patients on this organization. In the second group additionally, sufferers had been informed that humans might also or may not be praying for them. But no one prayed for this organization of patients. The 0.33 organization of sufferers had been told that humans were praying for them, and they were prayed for. The funding become $2.Four million for this look at. The question become, is there reduction in charge of complications and healing? The distinction in restoration and fee and degree of headaches become no longer seen in distinct corporations. I.E., the prayers did now not lessen danger of headaches or quicken the recuperation. In truth, the folks that have been prayed for had 18% occurrence of headaches like stroke while most effective thirteen % of the patients who were not prayed for has such complications.

In some other take a look at via Duke university, 750 patients who had cardiac surgical treatment deliberate were blanketed. The difference from the Tempelton look at became that the group had Christian, Jews, Muslim, and Buddhist affected person. The Study become multicentered and there has been no difference in the outcome of the coronary artery surgical operation in sufferers who had been prayed for and people who had been now not

So, the so-referred to as scientific records does no longer show that the prayers work. So, is there a problem with the studies or with the prayers? I even have a few remarks on these studies. Despite spending hundreds of thousands of bucks, the research were defective. In the Tempelton take a look at the prayers have been executed by means of 'paid devotee.' They did now not know sufferers, nor did they have any feelings for the sufferers and considering the fact that prayers are simply emotional there has been no 'connect' to the affected person or the God. 'Day care 'person's care can not be as compared to the care that a mother gives to her toddler. Paid devotee can not do prayer which can be going to be powerful. This is like scenario where I pray myself or ask a clergyman who's paid, to do the prayers for me after which me paying the priest for praying for my relative. The effectiveness is a great deal greater whilst 'first 'individual is concerned. The citizens of Briton definitely 'DON'T care 'for the longevity or health of British Royalty as tons as their family participants. The Long Live the King is said and not using a real attachment or emotions or devotion. It is just a mechanical component and that doesn't work. So, these studies are defective and can't prove that the Prayers carried out by oneself for oneself do not work. Once once more, the hassle is WE DON'T KNOW THE FUTURE or the so-known as future and so it's far extraordinarily tough to return to end. I will finish this with an antique tale to complicated in this point.

There were boys who were wandering via a jungle. They came throughout a temple. One of the lads turned into God Loving and so whilst he saw a temple he desired to head inner and pray. The other boy turned into atheist. He determined to not move in the temple. The first boy went inner, and he prayed, after praying he touched the ft of the statue of the God. A scorpion which became sitting on the toes of the statue, chunk his hand. The different boy who did now not go for the prayer turned into sitting out of doors and considering the fact that he had not anything to do, he was gigging the dust with a timber stick. He all of sudden noticed some thing and located a small pouch and whilst he opened it, it had some cash in it. So, you could conclude that the boy who became praying were given bitten with the aid of scorpion and one who did no longer pass in the temple and did not pray, got money. A priest arrived and so he treated the boy for the scorpion bite. The boy asked the priest that, 'I prayed the God and I get bitten by way of scorpion and this pal of mine does now not pray and receives cash. How do you give an explanation for that? 'The priest instructed him that' It is possible that if you had no longer prayed, then alternatively of getting dealt with for the scorpion chew and getting higher speedy, you might have died of scorpion chunk and if the opposite boy could have prayed, he could are becoming may be diamonds instead of small sum of money.' Since we do now not realize what the possibly final results is or what's the future, earlier than the prayer was executed, we do no longer understand if this explanation is accurate. But in reality, prayers make it less difficult to handle the horrific final results.

The Consciousness

We have pointed out the CONSCIOUSNESS in this newsletter commonly. The hassle that has been mentioned in neurology and in theology now a days is what's cognizance.

Everyone desires to realize what Consciousness is. And all and sundry has a solution after which many questions. The trouble has been discussed by many. But before we speak approximately that I want to explain the hassle that we never reflect onconsideration on but is there.

When I see an item, the mild rays or photons that comes out of a mild supply is contemplated from the item and that enters my eyes. The photons stimulate the retinal cells namely the rods and cones and then the impulse is going via the optic nerve into the occipital vicinity neurons behind the brain. And I then know that it a specific object – say table. If I observe a chocolate, then the photon debris replicate from the chocolate and do the equal system after which the SAME CELLS within the brain are stimulated. In one case I see a table and in different case I see chocolate and that causes one-of-a-kind feelings. In one case I need to consume the chocolate and in other case no such feelings. But how do I see desk in a single case and chocolate in other case. If the pathway is identical and the cells inspired are the equal, how is it that the impressions are specific. What is it that makes the decision that this is table and this is chocolate? The electric pastime or the chemical receptor interest is equal in all the cases, but the perception is distinctive. So how does that happen? Some might also say that when you take a look at an item, then the 'memory' reasons us to pick out one issue as table and other as chocolate. But how do electric or chemical pastime, that's identical in same neuronal cells, makes one-of-a-kind reminiscence stimulations. Certainly, the emotional reaction that happens while we see our pal versus a thief with gun in hand, is distinctive. So, how does that show up? How a chemical -electric pastime is perceived otherwise and in which is this saved? Let us take every other instance to raise a few other questions. Say I love pizza and so I see Pizza and I actually have preference to consume it and I consume it and I am satisfied. I want to eat 2d slice and so I devour it. But if I keeps to devour more and more, When I can be consuming — if possible and I even have now not thrown up via then the tenth slice will not supply me satisfaction but will deliver me ache and displeasure. So, what modified among 1st and 10th slice of pizza? So, is the satisfaction or happiness in eating pizza, in mind or in our thoughts? The same component is in track - opera or classical tune isn't enjoyed via every body. So, if the brain receptor stimulated are equal then why is the emotional response exceptional. Lastly a person can question me to think about morning dawn or event that befell years in the past, and I can convey it in front of my eyes right away. How does that manifest? If the solution is memory, then how is electric activity is transformed into snap shots or emotions and so forth.? How can identical chemical reactions in equal brain cells get translated into specific snap shots? Now reflect onconsideration on old character with dementia. If he looks at identical pizza and does not recall what it's far, he has identical cells stimulated in eyes and brain, however it does not motive any emotions or desires. So, the chemical reactions are the equal, but the response is quite exceptional. So, the chemical response by myself is not answerable for the emotions and intellectual reaction does now not happen despite the fact that there may be chemical reaction. So, we do need eyes and optic nerve and occipital lobe and the neurons there to be intact too, but we additionally need some thing greater and that appears to be thoughts and intellect and reminiscence. The neuroscientist will say that there's a storage of 'reminiscence' in other regions of mind- can be Hippocampus and while we see a familiar issue, the past reminiscence and enjoy will talk (? With whom) after which we apprehend that chocolate is to be eaten and enjoyed and desk is to place things on. And when those connections are severed then we do now not have memory. But nevertheless, that doesn't provide an explanation for what makes electric / chemical stimulation adjustments into an photograph of an object. But then what about the Consciousness- where does it fit in this? The cognizance pervades the whole thing – dead or alive but it is really an impartial observer and is needed for any of the opposite factors – mind -body – intellect. The recognition is wanted and can be answerable for the belief of various things as different things. This does happen thru the medium of thoughts and intellect and reminiscence, and we cannot understand whatever with out the tool of thoughts and intellect. But then we cannot perceive if we do no longer have consciousness. So, we need both thoughts- mind. One aspect of word that these things aren't a part of PHYSICAL BODY and so they persist even when the bodily body is not there.

The mind- intellect and physical frame are simple things and easy to recognize, we additionally recognise that at the time of death (of bodily frame) the mind and mind which might be a part of Astral frame or SUKSHMA SHARIR or also referred to as diffused frame, continues from one life to other lifestyles. But what is it that makes mind and intellect paintings? And we realize that the mind modifications and every person have own thoughts and unique intelligence. So, the consciousness is needed for working thoughts and intellect. But will we have ONE consciousness or will we have many- every one folks having different focus. The ADWAITYA Hindu philosophy feels that there is most effective ONE CONSCIOUSNESS.I do now not have a solution however sense that the recognition pervades the entirety and does not do some thing but without it we can't have any experience thru mind – mind. Since it pervades EVERYTHING, it is there whilst there may be no bodily body, however without physical body we can not judge if there is a reaction. The example that was given in past become that of energy. The energy while it flows via a fan it runs fan and whilst it is going thru AC, it cools the room and whilst it is going thru heater, it heats the room and when it is going thru a light bulb, it offers light. All this stuff can't do something without the power, however the power can not do something like light, warmth. Wind or cooling and many others., without the bulb,

Heater, or AC unit and so on. So, we want both elements, The same manner we want recognition and bodily body and diffused body and so on. Some feel that the recognition pervades EVERYTHING, and a few feel it's miles reflection of consciousness known as CHIDABHAS. Again, the recognition is some thing that can not be perceived and is nonchanging. So, we will feel the mind – intellect and of direction out bodily frame and so those matters aren't consciousness. One of the examples that has been given is that of glass bottles. If we get a few ocean water and put it in glass bottles and seal it and then placed it inner any other bottle and seal it and then positioned the ones two bottles in 1/3 bottle and seal it. Then we throw this in ocean. The water inside the bottle is same as the water in the ocean but the water inside the bottle remains from the water inside the ocean. If we can consider the outside glass bottle as the physical body and if we destroy it the water will still not be one with the ocean water. This is like death of bodily body. The external glass bottle is like physical frame

This is long past or broken on the time of dying, however the different two bottles are still intact – particularly Astral body or Subtle body and the Causal frame or KARAN SHARIR are nonetheless there and so the Consciousness is not one with everyday consciousness. Until we drop the 2 different our bodies or ruin the 2 different bottles, we are able to not be on with the focus which pervades the whole lot -much like the ocean water sealed inside the bottle despite the fact that same as ocean water throughout keeps the separate lifestyles from the regularly occurring focus. (This example isn't always perfect, and I know there are problems with this assessment, that is the near what I can recognize. This changed into given by Paramhauns Yoganand. The question still stays as to is it the Consciousness which is one and no longer many and the 'trapped' one in diffused frame and Causal frame is the mirrored image of the cognizance?

GENES AND LAW OF KARMA

Darwinian theory of evolution is widely recognized, and it has created many questions. Many Christinas agree with that the complete universe become created in 7 days and the God created it right away and there may be no evolution of Human beings from unmarried mobile organism. I had study a e-book titled" Language of the God" by way of Dr Francis Collins, questioning some components of the theory. He changed into leader of the Human genome project many years in the past. In 1840, Darwin declared that all of us have identical ancestor and to guide that announcement he furnished several examples. He had visited Galapagos Island. There he studied the fossils and other things and got here to the awesome conclusion that all Living matters on the planet have the SAME ANCESTER. WE ALL HAVE EVLOVED FROM THE SAME LIVING THING!

There are many humans in America that don't believe in the principle of evolution. Looking at a mouse I do now not feel that there was any similarity among mice and myself. But genetics says otherwise. In 2004 a query was requested to Americans as to which statement they trust or feel it is toward their perception.

1.Human beings are product of evolution from different creatures and God had a role in that process.

2.Human beings are fabricated from evolution from different creatures and God had no role inside the system.

three.Human beings have been created by way of God in final 10,000 years.

Forty-5 percent of responders agreed with option three announcement, thirty-8% agreed with alternative number1 and handiest 13% agreed for assertion wide variety 2. So even in advanced u . S . Like America humans do now not agree with in idea of evolution.